TOPICS IN AUTISM

Meaningful Exchanges for People with Autism

AN INTRODUCTION TO AUGMENTATIVE & ALTERNATIVE COMMUNICATION

JOANNE M. CAFIERO, PH.D.

Sandra L. Harris, Ph.D., series editor

Woodbine House ◆ 2005

All rights reserved under International and Pan American copyright conventions. Published in the United States of America by Woodbine House, Inc. 6510 Bells Mill Rd., Bethesda, MD 20817. 800-843-7323. http://www.woodbinehouse.com

The Picture Communication Symbols©, 1981-2005, Mayer-Johnson, LLC. Used with permission, Mayer-Johnson LLC reserves all rights worldwide.

Library of Congress Cataloging-in-Publication Data

Cafiero, Joanne.
  Meaningful exchanges for people with autism : an introduction to augmentative & alternative communication / Joanne Cafiero.
      p. cm. -- (Topics in autism)
  ISBN-13: 978-1-890627-44-7 (trade pbk.)
  ISBN-10: 1-890627-44-5 (trade pbk.)
  1. Autism--Popular works. 2. Autism in children--Popular works. I. Title. II. Series.
  RC553.A88C34 2005
  616.85'88206--dc22

                                                    2005015503

Manufactured in the United States of America

First edition

10   9   8   7   6   5   4   3   2   1

In memory of my brother,
Dennis John Cafiero. I will forever cherish
the meaningful exchanges between us.

Table of Contents

Introduction

Adam and Diane

Four-year-old Adam screams and throws himself on the kitchen floor. Adam's mom, Diane, sighs as she witnesses this all too familiar event. She has no idea what her toddler wants even after reciting a familiar list of things that usually quiet him down. "Do you want...a cookie...to watch a video...a drink...your Barney doll?" With the mention of each one, Adam's screams become louder and more frantic.

Last year, after numerous doctor appointments and evaluations, Adam was diagnosed with autism. A devoted and hands-on mom, Diane is becoming increasingly frustrated with her inability to understand her son's wants and needs and less tolerant of his tantrums. It's obvious that Adam's inability to communicate effectively is equally upsetting for him.

Tamika and Mrs. Myers

Tamika is a sixteen-year-old young woman with an autism spectrum disorder. In spite of years of systematic, consistent speech and language therapy, she is unable to speak. Tamika is in a special education life skills program at her local high school. She communicates using a few manual signs, vocalizations, and writing. Unfortunately, her handwriting is barely legible.

Tamika is an avid reader and has demonstrated an interest in above-grade-level literature. Her parents have requested that she be placed in an advanced literature class with her typically-developing peers for one period a day. But manual signs and illegible writing are not sufficient tools for interacting and participating in this class. Tamika's assistant, Mrs. Myers, is eager to work with Tamika but does not know how to support her expressive communication needs. Tamika is therefore isolated from her peers and the activity in the classroom. Tamika's inability to communicate not only negatively affects her participation in the class, but her behavior as well.

Michael and Zachary

Michael, diagnosed with Pervasive Developmental Disorder-Not Otherwise Specified (PDD-NOS), is an engaging seven-year-old with a "want to please" personality. Smiling broadly, he approaches his younger brother, Zachary, and gets within one inch of his face. Zachary backs up as Michael inches forward, making unintelligible sounds. Zachary yells to his dad, "Dad, Michael is bothering me!" Finally, Michael turns away, sits on the floor, and picks up an old catalogue. Holding the catalogue upside down, he flips through it, tapping each page before turning to the next one. Since it appears Michael desperately wants to communicate with his brother but can't do so in a way that Zachary can relate to, he resorts to unproductive stereotypic behaviors as an alternative.

Haley and Her Preschoolers

Haley is a special education teacher, fresh out of college. She is teaching in a preschool autism program in a large metropolitan area. Most of her six students are severely affected by their autism; few have any functional language, and their ability to engage and participate is very limited. Haley has a staff of two trained assistants, but even with this ratio, she and her staff are not able to teach and engage all the students simultaneously. Often, there are two or three students wandering around the room aimlessly, picking up toys and dropping them, or engaging in a variety of self-stimulatory behaviors, such as spinning the wheels of a toy car, head-banging, or staring at their moving fingers. The other children seem more interested in communi-

cating, but can't seem to time their efforts with the teachers' available attention. The school's administrators are not willing nor are they financially able to provide Haley with more staffing. Haley does not want a classroom in which the students interact only with the assistants and not with the teacher or their peers. Haley knows that each of her students harbors the potential to be a successful communicator, but she lacks the tools to unlock this potential.

Do you see yourself, your child, or your student in any of these scenarios? If you've picked up this book, it's likely there is a person with autism spectrum disorder (ASD) in your life negatively affected by his inability to communicate successfully. As a parent living with, or professional working with an individual on the spectrum, the everyday communication challenges described in the vignettes above probably sound all too familiar. Undoubtedly, you've witnessed countless melt-downs, like Adam's, resulting from your child's inability to get his meaning across or his difficulty understanding the communication cues around him. Like Mrs. Meyers, you've probably watched your student's communication attempts go unnoticed in a group, resulting in missed social opportunities. And like Haley, you're sure you've misunderstood your student's response to his environment or his peers, leading to less than ideal academic inclusion. You know how hard all this is on you; now imagine how difficult it is for your child or students!

The question you may be asking yourself is, "How can I engineer my child or student's environments and adapt language so that he can grow, learn, and achieve the best quality of life possible?" The answer is augmentative & alternative communication, also known by its abbreviation, AAC. In the past fifteen years, the quickly-evolving field of AAC has provided effective and exciting adaptations for people with all kinds of developmental disabilities, including autism spectrum disorders (ASD).

Augmentative & Alternative Communication (AAC) and Assistive Technology (AT)

Augmentative & alternative communication, referred to in this book as AAC, falls under the umbrella of assistive technology. Assistive technology, or AT, is a broad category encompassing any item, piece of equipment, product or system, whether acquired commercially off the shelf, modified, or customized, that is used to increase, maintain, or improve the functional capabilities of people with disabilities (Technology-Related Assistance for Individuals with Disabilities Act of 1988). Wheelchairs, grab bars, power scooters, ramps, eyeglasses, toys adapted with switches, and adapted eating utensils are all examples of AT. All AAC is a kind of AT, but not all AT is a type of AAC.

> **Assistive technology** is any item, piece of equipment, product or system, whether acquired commercially off the shelf, modified, or customized, that is used to increase, maintain, or improve the functional capabilities of children with disabilities *(Technology-Related Assistance for Individuals with Disabilities Act of 1988).*

So, what exactly is AAC and how does it fit in the assistive technology category? AAC is any tool, device, picture, word, symbol, or gesture that compensates for expressive (outgoing) and receptive (incoming) communication deficits. The tools, technology, and strategies of AAC serve to "increase, maintain, or improve" a person's ability to communicate by augmenting the skills he already possesses and providing alternative means when that degree of support is required. So, AAC is any type of assistive technology that helps a person with disabilities communicate. *AAC is never used to replace existing functional language, but to enhance*

> **Augmentative & alternative communication (AAC)** is a type of assistive technology. It is any tool, device, picture, word, symbol, or gesture that compensates for expressive and receptive communication deficits.

it. Remember however, communicating does not necessarily come in the form of speech. Communication is an exchange of information through virtually any means.

Unaided AAC are manual signs, gestures, and vocalizations. Using unaided AAC requires only your body, no external object or device.

Aided AAC are objects, three-dimensional concrete symbols, pictures, photographs, words, or simple line-drawn symbols.

AAC can include sign language, pictures, words, letters, or objects used either alone or in conjunction with communication boards, voice output devices, or keyboards. There are unaided and aided AAC systems. Systems, in this case, refer to the particular tools used with particular practices. Unaided systems include manual signs, gestures, and vocalizations. They require only your body, no external object or device. This book will briefly discuss using manual signs, a form of unaided AAC, and compare that system to the tools and devices of aided AAC systems. *The goal of this book is to provide an overview of aided AAC systems.* Aided systems involve an object, three-dimensional concrete symbol, picture, photograph, word, or simple line-drawn symbol. The tangible, visual symbols of aided AAC may be used alone or paired with a voice output communication aid (VOCA) or with computer applications.

Example of "no-tech" ACC

Aided AAC systems deliver messages through "no-tech," "low-tech," or "high-tech" AAC means. No-tech AAC are simple tools without batteries or circuits. No-tech can be a two dimensional card with a word or communication symbol on it,

Example of "low-tech" ACC

a communication wallet with multiple communication boards, or an activity-specific communication board. Using no-tech AAC, partners point to symbols or exchange them in order to communicate. Low-tech AAC devices are simple voice output communication aids (VOCAs) capable of playing back a few seconds to eight minutes of recorded speech. High-tech AAC devices are sophisticated voice output communication aids (VOCAs) with the capability of generating hundreds of messages. These high-tech devices can include

Example of "high-tech" ACC

portable keyboards with speech generating capability and even word prediction. More on these tools and devices will be discussed in chapter 3.

No-tech AAC devices are simple tools without batteries or circuits.

Low-tech AAC devices are simple voice output communication aids (VOCAs) capable of playing back a few seconds to eight minutes of recorded speech.

High-tech AAC devices are sophisticated voice output communication aids (VOCAs) with the capability of generating hundreds of messages.

AAC and Autism

A decade or two ago, AAC primarily addressed the needs of people with physical disabilities. Speech-generating devices would have been provided for people with cerebral palsy, for example, who were not able to produce intelligible speech. Regrettably, AAC's potential applications for people with autism were overlooked. Now, however, AAC is recognized as a powerful tool for individuals with ASD—in the home, classroom, workplace, and community. Some tried and true tools and strategies for teaching people with ASD that you are likely familiar with are types of AAC. These include visual schedules, visual prompts, communication boards. Picture Exchange Communication System, or PECS (Bondy & Frost), and sign language. This book will examine the use of some of these tools and strategies as well as other new, research-based and promising practices in AAC for people with ASD. We'll explore everything from three-symbol communication boards to five-dollar talking picture frames to 12K voice output devices that can store as many as seven thousand words!

Often, people with ASD have difficulty not only expressing language, but difficulty understanding language. They are challenged by difficulties with word retrieval and the complexities of person-to-person communication. On the plus side, people with

ASD often possess strong visual processing abilities. Because AAC is a visual communication medium, it's an ideal match for the specific skills and deficits common to people with ASD. Chapter 2 will explore the relationship between AAC and ASD in greater detail. AAC provides support for people with ASD in numerous ways and across many environments.

The Benefits of AAC

- AAC, as expressive language, facilitates connection to family and peers, and improves social skills.
- Through the use of visual supports, a person with ASD can better understand his environment and the routines and expectations within it. This lowers anxiety levels and results in more appropriate behavior.
- When a person with ASD has access to a functional communication system through AAC, he gains a measure of control over his environment and there's no longer a need for him to resort to difficult behaviors, like tantrums or aggression. With AAC, negative behaviors related to communication may be pre-empted before they become habitual ways of responding, and this preserves the dignity of everyone involved.
- Witnessing a person with ASD using language expressively through AAC often reveals hidden cognitive abilities and potential. Practitioners and parents who have experienced this note that with AAC-based expressive and receptive language supports, expectations are dramatically raised, and with that, more complex IEP objectives and vocational opportunities.
- Adapting curriculum and job procedures to function with AAC in school and the workplace allows the person with ASD more access and therefore more successful inclusion across all fronts.
- Effective communication enhances a person's positive self-concept, which in turn, increases his quality of life and the lives of those with whom he interacts.

About This Book

Throughout this book, AAC tools and strategies will be illustrated through real life vignettes of individuals with ASD. Each story will show how AAC enhances the lives of people with ASD by increasing their ability to communicate with others and thereby participate more fully in the world around them. You will notice that the case studies are always about two or more people, or communication partners: the communication partner(s) who can speak and the partner with language difficulties. This highlights the importance of understanding that AAC is about connection and interaction between people. The communication partner can be anyone: Mom, Dad, brother, sister, teacher, peer, bus driver, coworker, or whomever the person with ASD comes in contact with. The support and participation of the speaking communication partner(s) is essential.

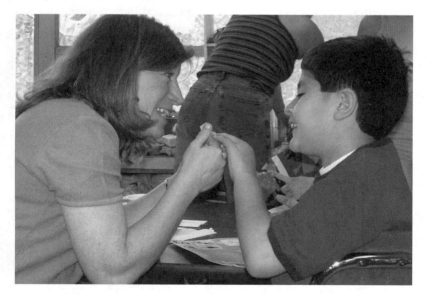

Chapters 1 and 2 of this primer will describe the learning styles and communication deficits and strengths of people with ASD. We will explore how AAC can meet those challenges and capitalize on existing skills. Brief research references will be provided to support AAC use for individuals with ASD, emphasizing that aided AAC does not inhibit speech in people with ASD, and, in fact, facilitates the use of speech. (Ganz, J., & Simpson, R. 2004; Broderick & Kasa-Hendrickson, 2001, Garrison-Harrell et al., 1997, Rowland & Schweigert, 2000, Charlop-Christy, Carpenter, LeBlanc, & Kellet, 2002, Mirenda, Wilk, & Carson, 2000; Dexter, 1998; Frost, Daly, & Bondy, 1997; Romski & Sevcik, 1996).

AAC tools, devices, and strategies for people with ASD will be described in chapter 3. We'll explore everything from the most simple communication board with a single symbol to the most complex high-tech assistive technology voice output device. Some of the AAC tools described in this book are very basic and can easily be made by parents and practitioners. Other AAC tools we'll discuss are inexpensive and readily available at your local electronics store. And some devices presented in this book are state-of-the-art AAC tools designed by manufacturers who continuously update them according to research and feedback from users and practitioners. Strategies for engineering your home, school, and community environments for optimal communication through AAC will also be addressed.

In chapter 4 we'll address the process of having your child or student evaluated for an AAC intervention. The assessment process determines the AAC tools and set of procedures best suited to the particular communication needs of a person with ASD. This chapter demystifies the assessment process by addressing how to get an appropriate assessment, who performs and participates in it, and provides sample assessments and answers to frequently asked questions.

Chapter 5 is devoted to special education law and what people with ASD are entitled to in the areas of assistive technology and AAC. This chapter will explain how to incorporate AAC into your child's educational program, funding options for purchasing AAC devices, how to ensure your child's communication system will transition with him when he changes schools or environments, and much more.

A recap of important points and brief discussion of the future of AAC concludes the book. Finally, an appendix will provide the information parents and professionals need to learn more about specific AAC devices and software. The appendix will include a list of manufacturers of voice output communication aids (VOCAs) and computer software, websites that provide free and useful information on AAC strategies, a list of useful AAC-related books and journals, and a compilation of conferences and annual training opportunities for parents and professionals.

This book is an overview of AAC for people with autism. I will not provide information on how to make tools, although some of the vignettes will be self-explanatory. Highly detailed descriptions of AAC devices are also not within the scope of this book. I will not prescribe a particular device for a particular type of communication deficit within the autism spectrum. A person with ASD's strengths and needs, communication partners, and communication environments should be carefully considered when pairing him with AAC tools and strategies. This is a highly individualized and dynamic process; as a student or child's life changes, so must his AAC. Therefore, parents and practitioners should not take a cookie cutter approach to matching their child or student with an AAC tool, device, or intervention. While two people may have the same ASD diagnosis and even similar behaviors, they will not have exactly the same set of skills and deficits. This is not meant to discount the value of observing what works with particular people and applying those principles to new AAC users; it is simply better to consider each individual a unique communicator with unique needs.

Who Can Benefit from This Book?

I wrote this book for parents, family members, friends, special and general educators, occupational and physical therapists, speech and language pathologists, clinicians, instructional assistants, and all practitioners who work with and care about individuals on the autism spectrum. The vignettes throughout the text reflect my personal experiences with students of all ages, some of whom once had little or no means to communicate, even labeled cognitively "not measurable." As an autism practitioner at Bittersweet Farms and a teacher in a public school classroom including students with autism I learned never to assume that a person cannot learn functional communication. I discovered that so many people with autism have great difficulty finding meaning in the ordinary events and activities of life. Hence it is essential that the vehicles by which communication are taught and learned are, above all, meaningful for the individual for which they are designed. This is where AAC comes in.

Thankfully, there are no cognitive, behavioral, or language prerequisites, or gatekeeper skills required for most AAC interventions. In other words, it doesn't matter where your child or student is on the on the autism spectrum, whether or not he has any functional speech, if he has mental retardation, splinter skills, or is cognitively more typical. If he has any difficulties understanding and generating language, or difficulties with word retrieval, AAC can help. If difficulties with language limit your child in any way, AAC can help. This help may be in the form of a simple written cue or as complex as a voice output communication aid. Regardless of the extent of the disability or the complexity of the AAC device, the AAC principles are the same: communicative input is visually augmented by the speaking communication partner and AAC tools are provided for visually augmented communicative output.

You might be happily surprised to learn that AAC has no target age-range; people of all ages can benefit from AAC interventions. For the youngest child with ASD, an AAC system can facilitate access to the very experiences that stimulate neurological development. For older children, AAC can stimulate cognitive development by providing the vehicle needed to access the school curriculum as well as social networks. Parents of young adults with ASD will find AAC can enhance their relationship with their adult child. AAC can provide support in vocational settings, not only for the practical facets of a job, but the social aspects of the work world. For people of all ages on the autism spectrum, whether they have had some or no prior experience with AAC, now is always the right time to start. In fact, after the introduction of AAC, practitioners report dramatic leaps in communicative competence, including initiations,  responses, increased vocalizing, joint attention, and experience sharing in adolescents and adults that had no previous AAC experiences (Cafiero, 2004, 2001).

While reading this book, you will discover that AAC can enhance an existing functional communication system or provide a communication system for a person where none existed. With very few exceptions, no readiness skills are necessary to begin using the first basic AAC tools. Never assume that a person with ASD is "too low functioning" to develop appropriate functional spontaneous communication skills. Often people with ASD who appear to be the lowest functioning or the most behaviorally disordered have the greatest potential as communicators and respond best to AAC. In fact, with the support of AAC, many of these individuals demonstrate a much higher level of cognitive functioning than observation or tests previously reported.

Perhaps you're under the impression that AAC is not worthwhile for your child if he is referred to as "high-functioning" or already has functional language. To the contrary, AAC not only provides an alternative way to communicate, it also augments whatever functional language exists and is often very helpful for verbal kids who have retrieval problems. AAC tools and strategies are shown to dramatically enhance the quality of life for people throughout the autism spectrum, regardless of the severity of their communication disability. In fact, any person with communication and participation challenges, even those who demonstrate some "autistic-like" characteristics, but lack a diagnosis, can benefit from AAC tools and strategies.

> The capability for interactive communication is an essential part of being human. Every person is entitled to the tools, adaptations, and devices necessary for functional communication.

It is my firm belief that children and adults with ASD and those demonstrating similar skills and deficits can reap huge rewards from the strategies and technologies available through AAC. The capability for interactive communication is an essential part of being human. Every person is entitled to the tools, adaptations, and devices necessary for functional communication. You will see for yourself that providing these tools for people with ASD to generate functional spontaneous communication can bring life-altering results. So, roll up your sleeves and let's get started.

1 | The Importance of Interactive Communication for People with ASD

Communication has been described as the core deficit for people with autism. In fact, one-third to one-half of all people with ASD will not develop speech that is adequate enough to meet their most simple daily needs (National Research Council, 1999). It is not unusual, for example, for a six-year-old with autism to learn to label hundreds of photographs of common objects by rote, but not be able to ask her dad for a glass of juice. Or for a teenager with autism to have basic reading and math skills, but be unable to tell her teacher she needs a break from an academic task.

The early signs of communication difficulties in ASD, seen in children as young as six months of age, manifest as a lack of pre-language behaviors, such as making eye contact, experience sharing, and joint attention with a caregiver. *Joint attention* is the ability to coordinate attention between a person and an object. When a child shows a toy to a parent or communication partner, or points to something of interest, she is demonstrating joint attention. Difficulties in joint attention affect our ability to focus on a partner, to share emotions, to follow the gaze of another person, and to draw attention to an object for the purpose of sharing an experience. These difficulties profoundly affect our ability to interact, preventing us from experiencing authentic socialization and building a social skills repertoire. Furthermore, a cascade of other skills typically build on these early social interactions. This simply does not often occur for many children with ASD.

Many people with autism also have difficulties with symbolic language. Spoken language and body language (gestures and facial expressions) are symbolic of feelings, ideas, wants, and needs. People with autism have great difficulty "reading" subtle nonverbal cues as well as direct verbal cues from others. The difficulties people with ASD have with joint attention and symbol use not only affect their ability to connect with others, but their ability to connect with their environment. These difficulties in connecting can result in confusion, anxiety, and frustration that can further lead to behavior difficulties. To illustrate, when a fire alarm goes off at school, a student with ASD who is unable to adequately read verbal and nonverbal cues may not understand the meaning of the alarm and the subsequent series of activities that prompts everyone to immediately leave the building. This sudden disruption of her schedule and her inability to express her fear or frustration may lead to inappropriate communicative behavior, such as aggression, screaming, or property destruction. So, an inability to read symbolic language can lead to problems, but successful communication and socialization provide access to more complex learning for all individuals. People with ASD have a critical need for the experiences and information that come from interactive communication.

Functional Spontaneous Communication

The National Academy of Sciences report, *Educating Children with Autism* (National Research Council, 1999), states that a priority goal in educational programs for children with autism should be the development of *functional spontaneous communication*. Being able to engage in functional spontaneous communication has been a predictor of positive outcomes for people with ASD (Garfin & Lord, 1986; McEachin et al., 1993).

Functional spontaneous communication can best be understood by looking at each of the three words. "Functional" means being useful, recognized by others as acceptable, and aimed at achieving a specific objective. For example, if a young girl with ASD desires a cookie, she will ideally say or manually sign "cookie" or point to a symbol for "cookie." A *non*-functional way to indicate her desire for the cookie, which results from her lack of communication skills and tools, is to have a tantrum or engage in self-injurious behavior. "Spontaneous" implies that communication, whether verbal or via AAC, is not cued, and in fact is in response to an internal, personal need or a natural environmental cue. Maria, a three-year-old girl with ASD wants to watch her Teletubbies™ DVD so she approaches her mother and gives her a small card with the picture of Teletubbies on it. If instead, Maria's mother sees her daughter pacing in front of the television and interprets her behavior by asking, "What do you want?" she has preempted Maria's opportunity to spontaneously communicate. Another example of spontaneous communication is one elicited by something in the environment. For example, Ty is having difficulty with a task so he approaches his job coach and signs "help." In this case, the difficulty with the task is the natural cue; Ty asking for help is a functional *spontaneous* communicative act. The third word in this phrase, "communication," refers to the exchange of information between communication partners.

Initiating spontaneous communication is a pivotal skill. That is, it provides opportunities for accessing more experiences that prompt more social and cognitive growth. A communicative initiation from a person with autism will most likely elicit a response from her speaking communication partner. That response can provide the stimulus for learning new language and social skills (Koegel, 1995). Although functional spontaneous communication is often initially absent in young children with ASD, this skill can be taught and when learned, outcomes for the children are more favorable (Charlop et al., 1985; Charlop & Trasowech, 1991). Recognized best practices and research-based functional communication teaching techniques for both verbal language and alternative forms of functional communication should be consistently used in all natural settings and environments of the person with autism (National Research Council, 2001).

As you can see, functional spontaneous communication is a critical skill and one that can make an enormously powerful impact on one's quality of life. Imagine not being able to communicate your need to use the bathroom or your desire for a delicious slice of birthday cake! AAC is an effective tool that can provide people with ASD the means to engage in functional spontaneous communication: to express what they need and how they feel. In this way, the world, for them, becomes a more responsive, kinder, friendlier place.

Do My Child's or Student's Communication Challenges Make Her a Candidate for AAC?

The criteria below describe some of the indicators for AAC. Take a look at the list. Do any of these apply to your child or student? The presence of any one or combination of these conditions makes your child a good candidate for AAC.

Does your child or student…
- Have no speech?
- Have delayed speech?
- Have unintelligible speech?
- Have a limited vocabulary (between one and twenty words)?
- Appear to be deaf?
- Use a word, phrase, or sentence once then never again?
- Use speech only to ask for a something highly desirable?
- Use requesting words (e.g., "I want") but not commenting words that are often abstractions, like "thirsty," "cold," or "the cookie tastes good"?
- Use language only by rote, repeating words or phrases she's heard (echolalia)?
- Have difficulty making requests?
- Have behaviors difficult to interpret?
- Not respond to questions?
- Have difficulty with short-term memory?
- Have difficulty initiating interactions?
- Have difficulty interacting with others?
- Communicate only about specific topics?
- Become upset and frustrated for unknown reasons?
- Become upset and frustrated for known, but seemingly irrational, reasons?

Communication is speech, body language, facial expressions, gestures, and written language or print. Communication can be *expressive*—i.e., what is said, mimed, or written, or *receptive*—i.e., what we think about and understand when we experience communication in its many forms. If a person has limited or no functional speech or language (expressive communication skills), and limited or no comprehension (receptive communication skills), AAC can provide the appropriate supports to enhance communication.

Communication is a primary behavior in human beings. We are born ready to give and receive information by gesture, sound, and touch. For this reason, the concept of "readiness" does not apply in the first simple and basic steps of AAC interventions. Of course, more complex AAC interventions involve being able to understand categories; others require basic literacy skills. In these cases, there may be some prerequisites. But it should never be assumed that a person with ASD does not possess those prerequisite skills. For example, there are people with ASD, even young children, who have precocious decoding skills for symbols, including text. These skills are often unknown to parents and practitioners and only emerge when opportunities with visual symbols, such as keyboards, word processing programs, and even pencil and paper are provided. So, the lesson here is try first and question later. A person is never *not* ready to give or receive communication. This book has a "zero exclusion" perspective: No individual with ASD, regardless of the difficulties with or even absence of communication, is excluded from consideration for AAC. In fact, *any* person with communication and participation challenges, even those without a diagnosis of ASD, can benefit from AAC tools and strategies.

> A person is never NOT ready to give or receive communication. Communication is a primary behavior in human beings. No individual with ASD, regardless of his difficulties with or even absence of communication, is excluded from consideration for AAC.

Can Adults with ASD Benefit from AAC?

The tools presented in this book address the communication needs of many, many people with ASD. And there is every reason to include adults with ASD who may have never had the opportunity to use AAC in any consistent way. Communication gains for adults with ASD can be every bit as significant and life changing as those for a preschooler. Developing better communication is an ongoing and  lifelong goal for all human beings, so it is important to consider providing adults with autism the opportunity to enhance their communication skills through AAC.

How Does AAC Affect the Development of Speech in People with ASD?

AAC is interactive two-way communication. AAC is used by both communication partners: the speaking partner, and the limited speaker or non-speaking partner. This means that the speaking communication partner will use the AAC tool along with her speech. In this way, the non-speaking partner is receiving communicative input both visually and auditorally. The non-speaking partner is better able to understand the communication because the visual component is easier to process for people with ASD.

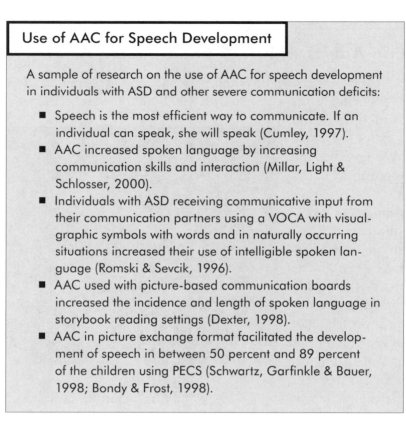

Use of AAC for Speech Development

A sample of research on the use of AAC for speech development in individuals with ASD and other severe communication deficits:

- Speech is the most efficient way to communicate. If an individual can speak, she will speak (Cumley, 1997).
- AAC increased spoken language by increasing communication skills and interaction (Millar, Light & Schlosser, 2000).
- Individuals with ASD receiving communicative input from their communication partners using a VOCA with visual-graphic symbols with words and in naturally occurring situations increased their use of intelligible spoken language (Romski & Sevcik, 1996).
- AAC used with picture-based communication boards increased the incidence and length of spoken language in storybook reading settings (Dexter, 1998).
- AAC in picture exchange format facilitated the development of speech in between 50 percent and 89 percent of the children using PECS (Schwartz, Garfinkle & Bauer, 1998; Bondy & Frost, 1998).

AAC enhances existing communication modes and is not meant to replace existing functional communication—that is, effective, appropriate communication through gestures, vocalizations, verbalizations, facial expressions, body language, or manual signs. There is no research-based evidence demonstrating that AAC interferes with the development of speech. This is important to note since many parents and practitioners fear that using AAC will prevent children from developing and using conventional speech. Research indicates that AAC actually facilitates speech by increasing communicative skills and interactions. Sign language in conjunction with speech has been shown to increase receptive and expressive language at a greater rate than speech training alone (Goldstein, 1999). Visual symbol systems, including tangible objects, pictures, and words have been used successfully with people with autism to increase communication and compliance, and decrease verbal prompt dependence (Mirenda and Santogrossi, 1985; Cafiero, 1998, 2001). AAC also provides verbal models for speech, either from the communication partner or the voice output communication aid (VOCA) (Millar, Light, & Schlosser, 1999).

2 | ASD & AAC:
The Perfect Fit

As illustrated in the chart on the next page, the features of AAC and the learning characteristics of individuals with ASD make a compelling match. Autism is a "spectrum" disorder, which simply means the people it affects experience a wide range of strengths and needs, splinter skills, and learning styles. Each person with ASD possesses a unique array of gifts and deficits that profoundly affects their connection to others and to the world. For this reason you cannot take a "cookie-cutter" approach to finding the right AAC intervention for your child or student. No two people with

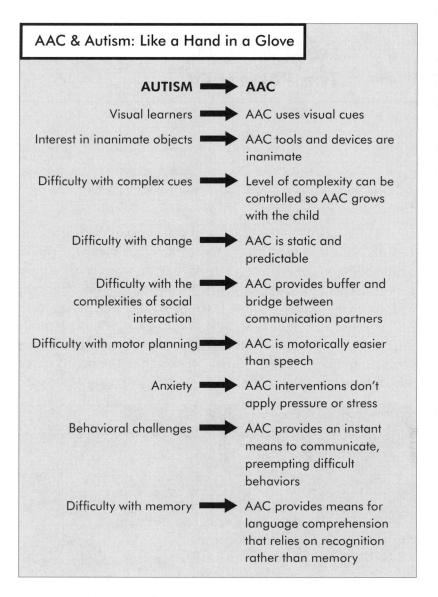

AAC & Autism: Like a Hand in a Glove

AUTISM ➡	AAC
Visual learners ➡	AAC uses visual cues
Interest in inanimate objects ➡	AAC tools and devices are inanimate
Difficulty with complex cues ➡	Level of complexity can be controlled so AAC grows with the child
Difficulty with change ➡	AAC is static and predictable
Difficulty with the complexities of social interaction ➡	AAC provides buffer and bridge between communication partners
Difficulty with motor planning ➡	AAC is motorically easier than speech
Anxiety ➡	AAC interventions don't apply pressure or stress
Behavioral challenges ➡	AAC provides an instant means to communicate, preempting difficult behaviors
Difficulty with memory ➡	AAC provides means for language comprehension that relies on recognition rather than memory

autism have the same combination or degree of skills and challenges, so matching AAC tools and devices to a person with ASD is a highly personalized process. Nevertheless, there is a correspondence between the features of AAC and the learning styles of people with ASD.

Visual Learners

First, most people with ASD have strong visual processing skills and much weaker auditory processing skills. Visual stimuli, like pictures and words, are permanent and not fleeting like sounds and manual signs. AAC relies on visuals, like objects (tangible symbols), pictures, photos, and written words to communicate thoughts and ideas. For people with ASD, the visual language on AAC tools and devices is easier to process than impermanent speech and manual signs.

Interest in Inanimate Objects

Children and adults with autism often show unusual interest in inanimate objects. For someone who dislikes change, an object, which is static and predictable, is appealing. AAC tools and devices are inanimate, predictable, and more static than speech, and people with autism often find them tolerable, even pleasant, and inherently motivating to use. And perhaps an inanimate object provides a comforting kind of sensory input for the person with ASD. Furthermore, people with autism often have difficulty relating to others and are more comfortable relating to objects. This may be because interacting with people is dynamic and involves processing multiple complex cues: speech, body language, appearance, tone of voice, and other things that may be going on in their surroundings at the time.

Trouble with Complex Cues

People with autism often have trouble processing complex cues, such as multiple step directions, speech, body language, and dynamic visual stimuli in a social interaction. Because they are unable to process a complex cue, they may "over-select" a

The Picture Communication Symbols©, 1981-2005, Mayer-Johnson, LLC. Used with permission. Mayer-Johnson LLC reserves all rights worldwide.

single, simple object or cue and focus on this irrelevant feature and literally miss the forest for the tree. This is a difficulty in what is called *multiple cue responding*. It is theorized that responding to increasingly more complex cues stimulates brain development in young children (Burke & Cernigila, 1991). AAC tools and devices can be created and programmed with simple cues (such as one symbol), then increasingly more complex cues (many symbols) as the communicator learns to understand and express more complex language.

Communication boards can be designed with the developmental level of the AAC user in mind. The communication board displayed above shows four different examples of AAC communication scripts to request a cookie, from the most simple, "cookies," to the four-symbol request, "I want more chocolate chip cookies." To request a cookie, a developmentally young communicator might point to or exchange a single symbol, "cookies," while another communicator with more developed complex language skills may be able to point to a series of symbols to express "I want more chocolate chip cookies." Using a communication board, another communicator may request a specific choice, such as an oatmeal cookie rather than a chocolate chip one.

Difficulty with Change

Sometimes referred to as an "insistence on sameness," most people with ASD have difficulty with changes to their routine and environment. To address this, the grouping of visual symbols on a communication board or voice output communication aid (VOCA) is static and predictable, as is the vocabulary and each symbol's placement on the board. New concepts and the new words representing them are added to the communication boards within the familiar framework of the existing symbols making the process less novel. All this adds up to a recognizable and comfortable means to communicate.

Difficulty with Social Interaction

The dynamic nature and multiple complex cues that are part and parcel to interacting socially can be anxiety provoking for people with autism. AAC acts as a safe buffer from the awkwardness and discomfort sometimes experienced by both the person with ASD and his communication partner. At the same time, it is a bridge between the two communication partners. Interacting with others gives us social information that is so valuable in the development of cognition and emotional intelligence. AAC can facilitate that development.

Trouble with Motor Planning

Many people with ASD have trouble with small muscle motor movements and motor planning. Motor planning is the ability to coordinate and sequence movements to accomplish a particular task, such as buttoning a shirt or writing with a pencil. Motor planning can affect a person's ability to coordinate and sequence the oral-motor movements necessary for speech. This neurological deficit may account for the difficulties a person with ASD has generating speech. Speech communication involves incredibly complex coordination of the tongue, mouth, and lips. Using an AAC device requires a simpler motor act, such as pointing to a symbol on a communication board, giving a symbol card to another person, touching a button on a voice output device, or using a keyboard.

Autism and Anxiety

Experiencing anxiety is common for people with autism. Using an AAC device is meant to be simple and efficient. AAC gives a person with ASD an easy way to communicate his needs. Pressure and stress are never a part of an AAC intervention and AAC is used to quiz or test an individual only under very special conditions. For example, if the AAC device is truly used by the person with ASD as his voice and ears, the AAC device may be used for doing homework, answering questions, or taking tests. However, beginning AAC interventions should *never* involve quizzing or testing.

Behavioral Challenges

Behavioral difficulties seen in ASD are often the result of an inability to communicate. When a communication system is not provided for someone with ASD, that person may develop challenging but nonetheless effective means to communicate, such as tantrums and aggression. AAC, when provided early on, will preempt the need for the development of these difficult and sometimes dangerous behaviors. Introducing AAC to a person who has already developed inappropriate communicative behaviors can help decrease those behaviors.

Difficulty with Memory

With the exception of people with Asperger's disorder, I have discovered in my own experience that many people with ASD have great difficulty mentally holding onto and retrieving chunks of information. AAC provides a communication bank of static symbols that allow the person with ASD to rely on recognition, rather than memory, to retrieve the words and messages they want to communicate.

AAC and Brain Development in Young Children

New theories in the area of brain development in young children provide further support for using AAC. The brain of a young child from birth to about age twelve is growing very rapidly in response to early experiences. All parents touch, coo, read, and sing to their little ones. Children who develop typically will seek out these experiences and soak them up like sponges. In fact, typically developing infants and toddlers will work hard to repeat enjoyable experiences as they learn cause and effect. Repeated experiences create neurological connections in the brain that support more complex learning (M. Johnson in Acredolo & Goodwyn, 2000).

But what happens when a child has ASD? Remember, many children with ASD have difficulty processing complex stimuli i.e., a storybook with many pictures or an interactive peek-a-boo game with Daddy, so they will naturally select simple, predictable experiences and stimuli, such as the wheel on a toy car or a piece of string. Some toddlers and children with autism appear to defy this characteristic and are attracted to letters and words and will focus on and appear to read printed materials. This precocious reading ability is called hyperlexia. While these children can read a variety of materials, they are not often able to comprehend what they are reading. The activity, although seemingly complex, is done in isolation and devoid of any functional, social, or interactive component.

Left to their own choices for stimulation, a child with ASD will only engage in a limited number and type of activities and therefore create limited neurological connections. They certainly will not reap

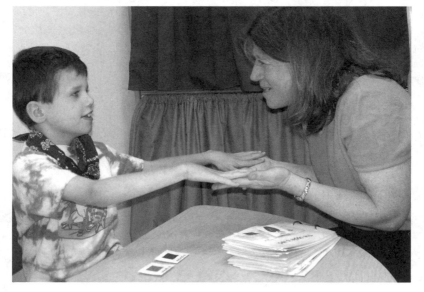

the benefits of complex play and social experiences. Even a child who has hyperlexia and is interested in print and appears to be reading, will only explore that skill in an isolated, non-interactive way. What is so problematic about this limitation in experience is that around the age of twelve the body absorbs or erases any under-used brain connections (Bransford, Brown & Cocking, 1999). This is where AAC comes in. AAC can be a vehicle for more complex learning by facilitating communication and participation in the work of growing up: play, interaction, experience sharing, and making simple and complex events occur (means/end behaviors).

The Benefits of AAC for Individuals with ASD:

People with autism, whether they have no speech or are limited speakers, can learn to communicate with AAC. Children and adults with autism have particular learning styles that are uniquely suited for AAC tools and devices. Providing the opportunities for people with autism to use AAC can release a cascade of positive life experiences and a more enhanced sense of self. The following is a list of AAC's potential benefits:

- May stimulate brain development
- Supports functional spontaneous communication
- Facilitates access to social information
- Facilitates inclusion at home, school, and in the community
- Facilitates greater independence in the home, school, and community
- Facilitates access to literacy experiences
- Preempts the need to develop aberrant communicative behaviors
- Provides a voice and ears to people with autism, including psychological benefits of better understanding others and being understood
- Facilitates an improved sense of self (self-concept) due to greater independence and fewer outbursts

3 | AAC Tools & Strategies

Linda and Ryan

Linda is a new first-time mom. Her nine-month-old son Ryan is sitting in his highchair. Suddenly Ryan lets out a loud squeal, "eeeeee," and Linda immediately makes eye contact with him. In a high pitched voice she says, "Hey Ryan, what's up?" Ryan looks at his mom, and with arms waving in excitement, makes another, different sound, "eeegooooog." To this Linda says, "Hey, you want to go outside in your stroller?" Ryan responds with another "eeegooooog." And with that, Mom says, "Outside? OK, my big boy," takes Ryan out of his highchair, puts on his jacket, and takes him outside.

Consider Linda and her son. How is Ryan learning language? Miraculously, human parents seem to be wired to do certain things like make sounds, say words, and make facial expressions and gestures that prompt reciprocal interaction from their babies. These behaviors, like cooing, smiling, and making eye contact, can be initiated by either baby or parent. This is early language and it is very important. Linda is intuitively shaping Ryan's cooing and gurgling into words by interpreting those sounds as language. Ryan is learning that the sounds he makes have the power to make things happen.

The typical infant like Ryan learns language by hearing it and by the responses he receives from the people around him when he is making speech-like sounds. Ryan is totally immersed in language and he will learn language, not from drill, practice, or flash cards, but by experiencing it. The language exchanges between Ryan and his mom are intuitively measured by both of them. Ryan makes sounds and Linda gives him short expressive sentences that are providing the framework for Ryan's later use of actual words.

Natural Aided Language (NAL)

This model of reciprocal give-and-take, and shaping communicative efforts into clear communication is the model used in augmentative & alternative communication. In the world of AAC, it's called Natural Aided Language (Goossens', Crain & Elder, 1992; Cafiero, 1995). Natural Aided Language (NAL) is an AAC strategy that utilizes the "mother tongue" method of learning language—the way we see Ryan and Linda interacting with each other. Natural Aided Language implies that communication partners are both giving and receiving language input. In AAC, language input and output are augmented with visual symbols. The speaking communication partner must provide the same kind of stimulation to his non-speaking communication partner that new parents provide for their babies. In NAL, control is shared by both communication partners and all communicative attempts of the non-speaking partner are acknowledged and responded to. Using this method, communicative interactions of both communication partners can be measured, analyzed, and adjusted for the purpose of stimulating more and better language.

The augmented input floods the environment of the person with ASD. Speech paired with visual symbols is the augmented input needed to start the process of introducing a "second language" into the environment. This second language is a visual language consisting of pictures, symbols, or written words paired with speech. Spoken language is the first language and visual language is the second language.

However, as mentioned in chapter 2, people with ASD often have difficulty processing complex cues, so flooding the environment with visual stimuli may seen contraindicated. It is important to remember that the cues you provide as communicative input should be measured and limited by the processing abilities of the potential AAC user. In other words, a person who has difficulty attending to a visual stimulus should initially be presented with only one visual cue. The intervention will involve adding more cues as the user is able to attend to greater stimuli. AAC can be customized to be as simple or complex as needed. A simple cue will provide the scaffolding for learning more complex cues. Remember, though, it is preferable to err on the side of providing too many, rather than too few visuals. Each visual cue is a potential unit of communicative input. Only when it is clear that the AAC user is not processing those visuals should the amount be decreased.

> **Natural Aided Language (NAL) is** a measurable total immersion visual language system in which the speaking communication partner pairs speech with pointing to symbols. NAL simultaneously teaches the non-speaking communication partner to both understand and generate interactive language.

AAC as a Second Language

Difficulties with motor planning account for some of the language deficits in people with autism; however, other things contribute to this difficulty as well. People with ASD do not receive understandable language input from conventional speech. Without receiving meaningful language input, they have great difficulty generating meaningful communicative output. In simpler terms, without understanding the words they're hearing and the gestures and facial expressions they're seeing, people with autism have trouble learning how to produce understandable language. This is where AAC can help. AAC *augments*, clarifies, or enhances existing communication modalities. This benefits people who have some receptive or expressive language but not adequate enough to meet their needs. The *alternative* in augmentative & alternative communication refers to communication that substitutes for speech.

Four Important Roles of AAC

1. To enhance existing functional communication by clarifying vocalizations, gestures, body language, etc.
2. To expand the language of limited speakers by increasing their vocabulary to include verbs, descriptors, exclamatory comments, etc.
3. To replace speech for people who are nonverbal.
4. To provide the structures and tools to develop language.

AAC augments existing functional communication or provides an alternative means to communicate by pairing a picture, symbol, or word with spoken language. This act of pairing is the dynamic model of AAC as a second language. This second language is best experienced by the non-speaking individual through total immersion (Abrams & Cafiero, 1991). The environment should be flooded with visual symbols in every place and scenario where there is a potential for communication: eating meals, playing games, going to the grocery story, reading a bedtime story, etc. Providing photos, line drawings, written words, and other visuals in a variety of environments not only unlocks existing language inside people with autism but encourages more language. Providing aided language stimulation, pairing speech with visual input, must be an ongoing process rather than a "one shot" intervention. Case study research, although limited, shows that the more visual and verbal input received by a person with ASD, the more expressive language she will generate. Other case studies and informal observations, although limited, report that when people with autism receive decreased visual receptive language input, their expressive language decreases (Cafiero, 1995, 2001).

Communicative Input and Output

Communication is both receptive (input) and expressive (output). What do we mean by this? Communication goes in two directions between partners: one person actively communicates (outputs) and the other person receives (inputs) that communication, and visa versa. AAC is both communicative input and output. One communication partner is expressing language using augmented output while the other communication partner is receiving language as augmented input.

Input and output for a non-speaking communication partner should be both visual and auditory. AAC assumes that the speaking communication partner and the non-speaking communication partner are **both** using AAC. This piece is crucial for AAC to be successful. The speaking communication partner is simultaneously interacting with his non-speaking partner and teaching the language through modeling its use. Many people wrongly assume that if a person with autism is provided AAC, she will spontaneously use it.

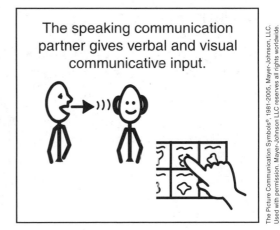

The speaking communication partner gives verbal and visual communicative input.

The language deficits in ASD are both in understanding and generating language. Therefore speaking communication partners *must* augment what they say.

> AAC is both augmented input and output. In other words, communication partners send communication and receive communication using AAC. Communicative input and communicative output are equal in importance.

Usually, first-time speaking communication partners have little difficulty learning to pair their speech with AAC. This means pairing speech with the essential words, rather than articles, prepositions, and other words that do not add any essential meaning. Although prior training or experience with the AAC tool or device is helpful, often using the tool or device is simple and intuitive. There are people with ASD who have some receptive language, especially for familiar words and phrases. In these situations it may not be necessary for the speaking communication partner to pair every spoken word with AAC. As a general rule, however, speaking communication partners should pair the key words in their speech with AAC.

Engineering Environments for Communication

Illustration of an Engineered Environment: Deshawn and Her Son Terrel

Terrel is a quiet two-year-old boy recently diagnosed with ASD. When left alone, Terrel sits on the floor and rocks back and forth. He makes whining sounds but does not use any understandable speech. When his mom and dad are home he will lift his arms asking for a swing. A picky eater, Terrel has a fondness for Goldfish® crackers. Terrel enjoys running outdoors and often opens the door and darts into the backyard.

Terrel's mother, Deshawn, meets with an early interventionist and together they target potential communication partners for Terrel as well as motivating activities. The early interventionist advises Deshawn to take two photos, one of Terrel's dad swinging him and another photo of the backyard. Deshawn uses a picture of a Goldfish from the cracker box to use as the symbol for eating crackers. Deshawn affixes the "crackers" symbol to the kitchen cupboard and the symbol for "backyard" on the back door. She places the "I want to swing" symbols in two different locations: one in the kitchen and the other in Terrel's bedroom.

Deshawn teaches Terrel to hand her the symbol indicating what he wants. Each time Terrel communicates a request this way, Deshawn models his request using her speech while pointing to the symbol. Terrel soon learns that these symbols represent cracker, outdoors, and swing. He seeks out these symbols and increasingly presents them to his mom and dad. Terrel's parents model his request, pairing their speech with pointing to the symbol, and promptly give him what he asks for.

As you can see, Deshawn has begun to engineer her home for communication. She has identified the things Terrel wants most and created visual symbols for them. Deshawn is using Terrel's desire for these favorite things as motivation for him to communicate. It is important to begin an initial AAC intervention within the context of an enjoyable and reinforcing activity for the new AAC user. Once the AAC user has become comfortable with this new language, it is easier to use AAC for more routine and less motivating activities. Deshawn takes advantage of the opportunity to provide Terrel with aided language stimulation by showing him a symbol, saying the name of the symbol, assisting him in handing her the symbol, then giving him what he requests.

An engineered environment supports high levels of communication and participation through AAC. When a visual language is considered a real second language in an environment and parents and practitioners understand that this language is the voice and the ears of the person with ASD, they will naturally structure the environment for many opportunities to communicate. Environments can be engineered to support both receptive and expressive communication.

It is important to remember that an AAC device + a non-speaker + a communication partner does not necessarily mean that communication will occur. Communication opportunities must be identified, a need to communicate must be created, and communication partners must be trained to provide these opportunities to the AAC user. In addition to identifying natural opportunities for communication, it is important to identify and eliminate barriers to communication.

Identifying and Training Potential Communication Partners

Potential communication partners should be made well aware that what is generated by AAC is real language and that it is the ears and voice of the AAC user. Provide opportunities for communication partners to use AAC to communicate to each other with the AAC tool or device.

Make communication partners an integral part of identifying potential communication activities and environments, selecting appropriate vocabulary, and creating communication boards. Make communication boards based on relevant and motivating topics to the speaking communication partners, such as "What I will do on school break."

It's useful to model communication strategies involved in creating communication opportunities. Have trainees videotape you implementing a communication board with a person with autism. Watch the videotape and observe where you created effective communication opportunities as well as where you were ineffective. Note also the communication behaviors of the non-speaking communication partner. Video new communication partners only after you have videotaped and critiqued yourself.

Supporting the Acquisition of Receptive Language

In an engineered environment that supports receptive language, centers, objects, activities, and learning tools should be labeled with visual symbols or words. For example, a person with autism can negotiate an environment labeled with visual symbols by matching symbols on his visual schedule with symbols at their locations. Engineered environments are then also literacy-rich environments. For some people with autism, literacy becomes the vehicle for functional spontaneous communication.

Visual Transition Tools as Receptive Engineering

An engineered environment has visual transition tools that assist people with autism in dealing with the passage of time or shifting attention from one activity to another. Activity schedules, visual closure systems, first-then tools, count-down boards, and transition boards are all examples of transition tools. These are no-tech input tools made of everyday materials, card stock, contact paper, and Velcro®. Examples of visual transition tools are shown on the next page.

School-Based Transition Board

First-Then Board

Strategies for Stimulating Expressive Communication

Engineered environments should have interactive, activity-specific communication boards and voice output communication aids (VOCAs) in each and every environment and activity. This ensures communication opportunities everywhere and enables people with ASD to express their needs and desires. For example, in an engineered preschool environment, there are communication boards in the dress up center, housekeeping center, snack table, and art table. Observe typical speaking communicators engaging in those activities and note the language being used. Embed choices within activities, for example, if you're making pizza, provide a variety of toppings that the communication partner must use language to select. Include that vocabulary on the AAC tool or device. When practitioners and parents make communication boards, they should be certain that they are readily accessible and have back-up copies for those times they are misplaced or lost.

Motivating Communication through AAC

The motivation to communicate is imbedded within the natural reinforcement of activities. It is important to begin AAC interventions with motivating activities that capture and engage the new AAC user immediately. Understanding how AAC works in a reinforcing activity makes using AAC for more routine or less motivating activities easier. In fact, commonly, once people with autism experience the power of visual language, they eagerly follow visual protocols for many familiar and novel activities and tasks.

Illustration of Using Motivation: Deshawn and Her Son Terrel (continued from above)

A few months into the therapeutic intervention, informal assessments indicate that Terrel has learned to use single symbols to make requests. The early interventionist and Deshawn decide to provide Terrel with more complex language stimulation. They select a Natural Aided Language intervention in bubble blowing play. Terrel is transitioning from single symbol requests to multiple symbols for receiving and expressing more communicatively.

Two-year-old Terrel is sitting at the table with his mom. Deshawn knows that Terrel loves playing "blowing bubbles" with her. She has made Terrel a blowing bubbles communication play-

mat. The symbols for blowing bubbles are arranged around the perimeter of the play-mat. (See figure below.) Deshawn starts by showing Terrel the bubble soap, but she does not open the bottle. She waits, then she points to the symbol of  *the word "open" and says, "We need to open the bottle." He knows what comes next in bubble play and Deshawn engineers the activity so that Terrel's communication, (gesturing, pointing to symbols, or vocalizing) makes things happen. Throughout their play, Deshawn waits expectantly to stimulate Terrel to communicate. When Terrel pops a bubble with his fingers, Deshawn says, "Pop! You popped the bubble," while pointing to both "pop" and "bubble" on the play-mat.*

Each time Terrel attempts to communicate, Deshawn acknowledges, shapes, and expands his communication by pairing her speech with pointing to the corresponding symbol. When Terrel points to "more," Deshawn responds with, "More bubbles. I am going to blow more bubbles," to expand Terrel's communication. The vocabulary on the play-mat provides the language stimulation for a variety of bubble activities: blowing, popping, cleaning up spills, and also making comments, such as "Uh-oh" and "Yeah!"

Creating a Need for Communication

Communication opportunities should be created thoughtfully and deliberately. Central to engineering environments for communication is knowing what motivates people with ASD. Activities with both personal motivators and routines are full of communication opportunities. There are specific personal motivators for each person with ASD. For example, Taylor loves to use bright colors when drawing. Her teacher gives her a piece of paper and only one crayon. Taylor is highly motivated to use AAC to ask for more colors.

When engineering the environment, a parent or practitioner sets up situations where the AAC user must communicate to complete an activity, find an object, or correct a problem. In these instances, some independence is sacrificed for the sake of developing communication skills. For example, Patrick may already know how to make a peanut butter and jelly sandwich independently. His dad decides to put the peanut butter in a different place in the kitchen. Patrick then has to use his AAC device to ask his dad for help finding the peanut butter.

Besides personal motivators, a majority of people with ASD are motivated by familiar structured routines. Familiar routines can be effective motivators for communication. For example, Casey has learned to feed her dog. The routine involves getting the dog dish and the measuring cup, taking the lid off the dog food canister, and putting two cups of food in the food bowl. Casey's mom has "sabotaged" the routine by taking the measuring cup out of the dog food container. Casey must then use her AAC to ask, "Where is the cup?"

Teaching by Modeling

The primary role of the communication partner is just that: to be a communication *partner*. The language stimulation provided by the communication partner ought to be natural and without pressure. The speaking communication partner does not force their non-speaking partner to communicate, nor should they demand a long message string. For example, Kyan, a special education teacher, is having lunch with Jamar, a nonverbal boy with autism. Jamar has a large communication placemat. Jamar asks for help opening his milk carton by pointing to "help" on his communication place-mat. Kyan acknowledges his request by saying "Oh, you want help opening the milk" while pointing to "want," "help," "open," and "milk." She does not demand that Jamar point all four words before she helps him. She is providing the stimulation to use the words by modeling them.

The direct modeling of the speaking communication partner in natural environments is the most effective way to teach the use of AAC. Opportunities are naturally embedded within the environment and the activities that the AAC user must do within it. For people with autism, learning to use AAC in natural environments is particularly important because they have great difficulty generalizing what they learn outside of their training environments. The real world with real communication partners provides the perfect training opportunity. Research has shown that AAC users who have more opportunities to communicate are better communicators (Sigafoos, 1999).

Avoiding Prompt Dependence

It is the goal of this book to teach and promote interactive communication with a strong focus on the communicative input of the speaking partner. However, it is my opinion that communication partners should avoid the use of physical prompts, or "hand over hand" with their non-speaking partners. These prompts are difficult to fade. People with autism tend to link the physical prompt with the communication itself and have great difficulty communicating without it. They expect to have their communication partner's hand on theirs or will hold the finger of their communication partner and use it to point to symbols or letters.

In my experience, physical modeling is the most appropriate form of "prompting" since it is subtle, conversational, and requires no fading. For example, a speaking communication partner may ask a question using AAC, "Do you want a cherry or a grape popsicle?" and after waiting for a response and not receiving one, will answer with a statement, "You like grape," pointing to "grape" on the communication board. This is considered a kind of conversational prompt. There are other situations where very specific and subtle prompts can be used. If a communication partner is asking a question, she may point to the answer after waiting for the non-speaking partner to respond. A point prompt is easy to fade and can be used occasionally. However, it is important to maintain the interactive conversational style of the communication by giving input as well as output that is natural.

While it has been my experience that natural, conversational modeling is the most appropriate form of prompting, some physical prompting in AAC can be effective if faded. In teaching through the use of PECS, for example, a silent "ghost" trainer physically prompts the AAC user from behind and is almost invisible to both communication partners. This type of prompt can be helpful because the "ghost" prompter can actually feel when the AAC user is motorically engaging in using the AAC device or tool and can fade accordingly.

An easy-to-use, efficient prompt hierarchy has been designed by Janice Light and Cathy Binger and described in their book *Building Communicative Competence with Individuals Who Use Augmentative and Alternative Communication* (Brookes Publishing, 1998). This simple, but elegant hierarchy begins with natural cues as the first "prompt." The natural cue is the presence of the AAC and a typical situation that usually causes something to happen. The communication partner is directed to follow a prescribed sequence of subtle to more explicit prompts. The aim of this prompting sequence is to provide the non-speaking communication partner enough "wait" time to respond if they are able.

Experienced AAC practitioners for people with ASD have developed the "art" of using AAC and use Natural Aided Language with some subtle point prompting without cycling through a complete prompt hierarchy. It is important not to make the prompting procedures take precedence over the interaction and meaningful exchange between the two communication partners. Sometimes, an over-reliance on following a prompt hierarchy makes communication stilted and boring, with more of the features of a drill than of an interaction.

Inadvertently Preempting Communication Opportunities

Demanding long grammatically correct sentences to communicate when one or two words are sufficient can make communication cumbersome and inefficient. While there has been no research done specifically on this issue, there are anecdotal reports of children with autism who have "turned-off" to their AAC tools because their partners made the process so difficult. Communication for people with ASD needs to be as easy and efficient as communication is for speaking communicators.

In addition to this, many dedicated and well-meaning parents and practitioners inadvertently create obstacles to communication by preempting any need for language. This can happen by anticipating the needs of an AAC user, inadvertently removing her motivation to communicate. For example, Lian may automatically zip up her son Chen's jacket without giving him the opportunity to ask for help. Tom, a special education teacher, may put Trevor's favorite electronic game on the classroom game shelf where Trevor can access it without using language. If you notice that your child or student is using her AAC less than you might expect, examine your behavior and the environment for things that may be preventing communicative attempts.

Measuring Outcomes

It is important to be able to measure progress in any intervention, and an AAC intervention is no exception. Relying on your memory of AAC performances is often colored by your feelings and can be inaccurate. Quantitative data can give information regarding the effectiveness of both the speaking partner and the non-speaking partner.

Parents and practitioners can measure the effectiveness of an AAC intervention by charting communication initiations and responses using AAC. Other behaviors that can be measured as functions of AAC interventions include: how much time she is engaged, how quickly she follows a direction, what level of prompting she requires, and how independent she is without prompts. This data can assist a parent or practitioner in fine-tuning an intervention to increase a student's time on task and for more effective troubleshooting. Consistent, careful data collection prevents personal perception from clouding actual results. Without hard data it's difficult to quantify the effectiveness of an intervention for the purpose of justifying the expense of an AAC device. It's also hard to know when it's time to take the next step to a more sophisticated device.

Illustration of Data Collection: Deshawn and Her Son Terrel (continued from above)

The early interventionist helps Deshawn set up a simple data collection system to measure the number of words Terrel is using to communicate over a four-week period. Deshawn makes the bubble activity part of her daily routine with Terrel and counts the number of symbols Terrel is using each Friday. Each week, Terrel is pointing to new symbols as he plays bubbles with his mom. He is sharing control with his mom within the bubble blowing activity and is learning new vocabulary through a reinforcing activity.

There are many methods used to measure the effectiveness of an AAC intervention. One relatively simple way to quantify an AAC intervention is to measure vocabulary use, or the number of symbols the non-speaking communication partner uses to communicate. This can be done quite easily by making a copy of the communication board to use as a data collection tool. Once weekly, during the chosen activity, the speaking communication partner can write a number representing that week within the cell of the symbol that the AAC user used appropriately. In the data collection form shown below, Ter-

Terrel's Vocabulary Use:
Four-Week Probe Using "Bubble" Communication Board

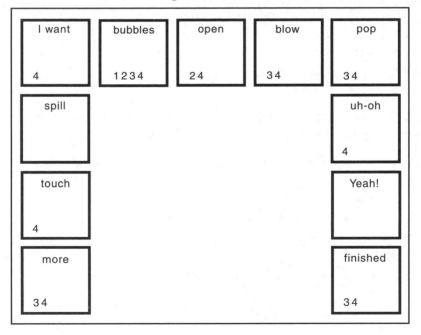

I want	bubbles	open	blow	pop
4	1 2 3 4	2 4	3 4	3 4

spill				uh-oh
				4

touch				Yeah!
4				

more				finished
3 4				3 4

rel pointed to the cell containing the word "bubbles" only once during the first week of data collection. It appears Terrel pointed to "bubbles" each time data was collected over the course of the four week data probe.

Over time, the number of symbols used can be counted and graphed so that if needed, adjustments can be made in activity format, vocabulary, or language stimulation to promote more communication and participation. When Terrel's weekly probe data is graphed (see below), it is clear that over the course of four weeks Terrel used increasingly more vocabulary and interacted more with his mom.

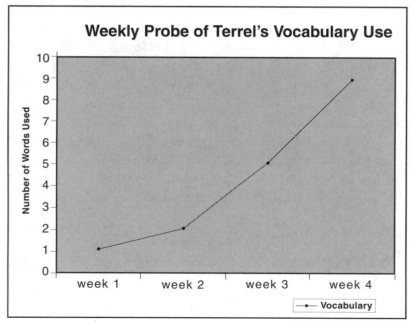

AAC Tools and Strategies as Best Practices

It is important to note that AAC supports are often used for people with autism as part of standard best practices in special education. These supports are less individualized than a dedicated tool or device and are often part of the classroom structure or general environmental adaptations. These supports include visual schedules, visual cueing tools, and visual exchange procedures, such as the Picture Exchange Communication System (PECS). This last technique is extremely useful and explained in detail in the book *A Picture's Worth: PECS and Other Visual Communication Strategies in Autism* (Woodbine House, 2002) by the developers, Andy Bondy and Lori Frost.

Visual schedules are objects, photographs, line drawings, or words representing specific activities and arranged linearly according to when these activities occur. They are visual reminders of what has passed, what is now occurring, and what will occur in the future. Often visual schedules include a visual closure system, which is any physical tool, device, or format that visually removes the symbol representing the completed activity from the schedule. This can take the form of a check-off list or "finished pocket" in which to place the completed symbol. Visual schedules are extremely effective for people with autism. Detailed information about how to design and implement them can be found in *Activity Schedules for Children with Autism: Teaching Independent Behavior* (Woodbine House, 1999) by Lynn McClannahan and Patricia Krantz.

Visual cueing tools are used to augment verbal instructions and cues. Visual cueing tools can take the form of symbols, manual signs, or written words. One can be used, for example, for a teacher to indicate to her class that it's time to line up at the door.

AAC Systems

The "standard best practices" tools and strategies discussed above are only a small part of AAC for people with autism. AAC includes many systems—sets of rules or protocols—that are used in the natural environment, such as Natural Aided Language (NAL) (Cafiero, 1995), which we discussed earlier in this chapter. If you recall, this system views visual language as a real interactive language and pairs speech with key visual symbols as both receptive and expressive language training. Many children will do extremely well with Natural Aided Language as a first AAC strategy. They will receive input from their communication partners and learn receptive and expressive language from that experience. They understand the symbols and can discriminate one from the other. Some beginning AAC users will learn the meaning of the symbols in a very short period of time. Other children learn from the more structured prompting of picture exchange.

The Picture Exchange Communication System, or PECS, is a strategy designed to be taught in six phases. First, the person with ASD is taught to initiate communication by giving a visual symbol for a highly desired item to a communication partner. She is then given that item in exchange for the picture, photo, line drawing, etc. Second, picture use is expanded to include more people, places, and rewards that the person with ASD might want to request. In the third phase, the person is taught to make specific choices between pictures. The fourth phase involves teaching the person to construct simple sentences with pictures, such as "I want truck." Responding to the question "What do you want?" is addressed in phase five, while in phase six the person is taught to develop conversational skills by commenting on various items and activities for social reasons, not only to get a tangible reward.

There are other AAC strategies used for people with autism and all use a naturalistic approach to language development. The System for Augmenting Language (SAL) is a strategy similar to NAL in that the speaking communication partners provide communicative input as well as output to their non-speaking communication partners in natural settings. In SAL, however, the communication is conveyed through the use of a voice output device (VOCA). Research demonstrates that participants in SAL training generate messages using multiple symbols, increase their symbol vocabulary, and increase the intelligibility of their spoken words (Romski & Sevcik, 1996).

Functional Communication Training with AAC (FCT with AAC) is a specific protocol designed to decrease problem behaviors. FCT has two important parts: first, to find out why a particular behavior is occurring, or what the person is trying to communicate with the problem behavior; and second, to teach a more appropriate way to communicate (Mirenda, 1997). For example, Chris continuously grabs french fries from the plate of his classmate, Andrea. His teacher prepares a VOCA with the message, "May I have some french fries, please?" and teaches Chris to ask for french fries by activating the VOCA. When he does so, his request is honored and he gets some french fries, thus reducing the need for the negative behavior.

AAC Tools and Strategies in Action

In light of the fact that AAC for people with ASD is so new, parents and practitioners need to be flexible and open as they negotiate the often overwhelming maze of AAC tools and devices. Stay informed and don't always depend on AAC specialists for updates on AAC technology. This field is advancing so rapidly that it is virtually impossible for one person to have the latest information on all the new technologies. The Internet is a great source of information. The appendix of this book also contains a reference list of electronic and conventional resources.

The following is a run-down of many of the current AAC systems and devices. Remember, the goal of this book is not to teach you how to use AAC, but rather what it is and why it is appropriate for your child. Read through this section with an eye for which strategies and tools you think will match your child's unique set of skills and deficits, then consult with the your child's team of professionals to set up an appropriate intervention strategy.

Unaided AAC

Sign Language and People with ASD

It is important, before we proceed with more complex AAC, to address the issue of manual signs. Manual signs are a form of "unaided" AAC. Unaided simply means that there is no external tool or device required to augment the speech communication. If the augmented input is in the form of manual signs, then it is important that the speaking communication partner sign *and* speak during all work and play activities. Other forms of unaided AAC are gestures, vocalizations, and tactual reception of signing where a deaf-blind person places a hand on the dominant hand of the signer so that she can "feel" the signs.

Sign Language Vs. Visual Symbols (Aided AAC)

Some people with ASD benefit from sign language while they are learning speech and will use more speech while they are signing. At this time there is very little research that compares the effectiveness of sign language over visual symbols as communication aids for individuals with ASD. Many parents and practitioners know, however, that there are people with ASD who successfully use many different forms of AAC, such as manual signs, picture symbols, gestures, and VOCAs depending on the situation, the environment, and their communication partners. Nevertheless, it is unusual to find an individual with ASD who learns more than ten signs expressively or uses them fluently and in a way that is understandable to her communication partners. Motor deficits and motor planning difficulties in people with ASD may account for their difficulty using sign language accurately and effectively.

Manual signs, however, are certainly more portable and less cumbersome than using symbols on communication boards. Manual signs offer unlimited vocabulary options. And it is more likely with manual signs than with aided AAC that an individual with ASD will be in physical proximity to her communication partner. However, limited research has found that in comparing the use of sign language with Picture Communication Symbols, PCS© (Mayer-Johnson, 1981) in individuals with ASD, the PCS were more intelligible to unfamiliar communication partners (people in the community). The chart below summarizes the case for both sign (unaided AAC) and pictures or words (aided AAC) (Mirenda, 2003).

Signs	Pictures/Words
Portable, always available	Language board or symbol required
Stimulates speech in some individuals with ASD	Stimulates speech in some individuals with ASD
Fleeting and temporary	Concrete and permanent; organizes information
Motoric competence required	Motorically easier
Not readily understood by unfamiliar communication partners	More easily understood by all communication partners
More difficult for communication partners to learn and understand	Easier for communication partners to learn and understand
Unlimited vocabulary	Vocabulary limited in most aided tools and devices

Aided AAC

Symbol Systems

Aided AAC systems include representational systems and tangible systems. Representational systems, like the one used in the

Deshawn and Terrel case study above, use two-dimensional symbols and include photographs or line-drawings, such as Picture It® (Slater Software, 1994-2005), PixWriter® (Slater Software, 1998-2005), and Picture Communication Symbols (Mayer-Johnson, 1981). Tangible systems are objects; partial objects, such as a small piece of towel to represent "wash hands," or miniature objects; textured symbols, such as bristles of a brush glued on a card to represent "brush hair;" and adapted line-drawn symbols with raised contours that can be identified by touch. Tangible and tactile symbols are used with people who have visual or cognitive deficits and for whom the line-drawn symbols are too abstract (Rowland & Schweigert, 1990).

The most widely used AAC symbol system in the United States is Picture Communication Symbols, or PCS. The PCS libraries consist of over ten thousand pictured words translated into forty languages. Each picture is presented in a visual box, or cell, and includes the corresponding word. The PCS libraries can be purchased in dictionary form or a computer program called Boardmaker®. Boardmaker is made in both Windows and Macintosh platforms. Boardmaker has add-on components, one that provides animated symbols and another that provides a talking feature for the symbols. Writing with Symbols 2000® is a talking picture and word processing program using Boardmaker symbols.

Picture It and Boardmaker are both available as software and are two of the most commonly used representational symbol systems in the US. In both Boardmaker and Picture It, you can import photos to personalize your communication tools. Below and on the next page are samples of the phrase, " I want to go home" in Picture It and Boardmaker.

The symbols below were generated by Picture It software.

| I | want | to | go | home |

Picture It® (Slater Software, 1994-2005)

This is the same message made with PCS symbols in Boardmaker.

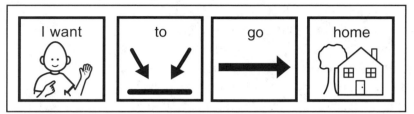

The Picture Communication Symbols©, 1981-2005, Mayer-Johnson, LLC. Used with permission. Mayer-Johnson LLC reserves all rights worldwide.

Voice Output Communication Aids (VOCAs)

Besides symbols, VOCAs are another type of aided AAC. They are either low-tech, i.e. capable of eight minutes of recorded speech or high-tech, more sophisticated machines that can generate hundreds of messages. VOCAs will be described in more detail in the section on AAC devices below.

AAC Devices

AAC devices are the concrete tools that are used as vehicles for AAC symbol systems. There are no-tech, low-tech, and high-tech communication tools and devices.

No-tech Devices

No-tech tools are used in the Picture Exchange Communication System (PECS), and as behavioral cueing tools, visual activity schedules, and multiple symbols or words on theme-based language boards, such as communication placemats and play-mats. Using no-tech AAC, partners point to symbols or exchange them in order to communicate. In fact, using paper and pencil to exchange messages can be a form of no-tech AAC.

No-tech tools have no batteries, electronic components, or voice output. They are created from symbols, photographs, pictures, or objects, and with everyday materials like cardboard, glue, and contact paper. They are easily made and ready to use. For example, a tangible or object-based symbol, such as a Goldfish cracker can be glued to a piece of cardboard, covered with clear packing tape, and paired with a one-dimensional PCS symbol for "fish cracker." Pairing is useful for helping the person with ASD ultimately transition  from a concrete system to a more abstract symbol only system, which is more portable and practical. This no-tech AAC tool can be used with non-speaking communication partners who aren't able to understand line drawings or photographs but relate better to concrete objects.

Using Symbols to Create No-tech Personal Communication Systems

Symbols can be arranged on interactive communication boards by subject or activity. These no-tech, activity-specific communication boards can be in the form of placemats, play-mats, or placed in a binder or wallet and tabbed for ease of use. People with ASD can be taught to locate the communication board they need through the modeling of the communication partner. It is important to note that having a leather-bound binder with colorful, laminated communication boards that is either kept on a shelf in school or in a closet at home is not a viable AAC tool. It must travel with the AAC user throughout her day.

Illustration of Combining No-tech AAC Strategies: Haley and her Preschoolers

Haley is a bright, "fresh-out-of-college" special educator who has been assigned to a new intensive preschool program for children with autism. She has been trained in PECS and the Natural Aided Language strategies and she is not certain how and when to implement these strategies and which students will need which strategy.

Haley decides to make snack boards with moveable symbols for picture exchange and fixed symbols for input. (See figure below.) In this way, she can provide receptive language input using Natural Aided Language and the children can exchange the PCS to request their snack choices. She can now communicate with her students by pointing to the symbols while she is speaking. The students can request what they want for snack by exchanging the symbol for the snack they want. To make the most of this communication activity, Haley has two edible snacks and two drink choices. Some of her students are using exchange to make requests, others are pointing to symbols to indicate their choices. All the students are receiving visual language input from Haley through their communication placemats.

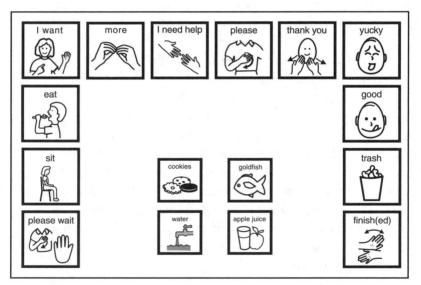

Just as speaking communicators use a variety of ways to communicate, such as speech, gestures, and writing, people with ASD can use multiple systems: manual signs, Natural Aided Language, PECS, and VOCAs according to their needs and the demands of the environment. In the story above, the special educator made a communication tool that combined two strategies and found that it addressed the communication needs of all six of her preschool students. No-tech, low-tech, and high-tech tools are often combined to create the best, most functional total communication program for people with ASD.

Low-tech Devices

Low-tech AAC devices are simple voice output communication aids (VOCAs) capable of playing back a few seconds to eight minutes of recorded speech. These electronic communication devices produce spoken messages when the user activates them through touch. There are a wide variety of these, some of which can be purchased at local electronic stores relatively inexpensively. New, more effective and user-friendly AAC voice output devices are being developed continuously and it is the intent of this book to provide a good cross section of the most popular devices. Talking memo switches, talking picture frames, and talking photo albums are all examples of easily purchased voice output tools that when paired with visual symbols become good AAC systems. These are programmed by simply recording a message on the device and mounting the corresponding symbol onto it. Talking photo albums, for example, with photographs or pictures and corresponding recorded text can become a reinforcing and inexpensive talking book.

Amanda, in the story below, is using a single switch VOCA (one touch generates one message). These devices are easy to use and particularly fun in joint storybook reading between a parent or teacher and a child. A repeated line from a story is recorded on the device and the child becomes a real participant in shared reading when she presses the button.

Illustration of Low-tech Voice Output Communication Aid (VOCA): Amanda & Jacob

Jacob, a five-year-old with Pervasive Developmental Disorder (PDD) is wiggling restlessly next to his mom, Amanda. Amanda is attempting to engage Jacob in an Old MacDonald storybook but he wants to get down off his chair and continue circling around the kitchen table. She has a Big Mac™ (a single switch AAC device) with a PCS of a child singing taped to it. She has recorded Jacob's older sister's voice singing "EiEiO" on the VOCA. As Amanda reads and presses the "EiEiO" button Jacob's wiggling stops. She continues to read and when it's time for the refrain she points to the Big Mac.

Jacob looks, touches the Big Mac, and with a look of surprise, settles down, listens to the story anticipating when it's time to sing "EiEiO."

There are several types of low-tech communication devices from the single switch mentioned above to a single switch with the capability of saying a sequence of multiple messages each time the device is touched (Step by Step Communicator™). There are low-tech devices with anywhere from one cell for one message to up to thirty-two cells for thirty-two words or messages. In addition

to the variability in the number of messages a device can hold, low-tech AAC devices may also have "levels." Levels provide the capability of recording multiple individualized activity-based vocabulary sets for several environments or activities. These devices have memory allowing them to store each activity-specific series of messages. The communication partners can switch from one activity to the next by changing levels on the device. Communication partners simply turn a switch and insert the appropriate communication board into the overlay (communication board) slot.

No-tech Vs. Low-tech AAC

VOCAs have several advantages over no-tech strategies and tools. First, they can be more reinforcing and motivating for some children than mere symbols. In storybook reading, a VOCA enables the student to become an integral part of a shared reading experience. In day to day communication, a message on a VOCA can be heard; with a no-tech symbol, the communication partner must be in close proximity to see what her non-speaking communication partner is "saying." Some VOCAs have built in handles for carrying; others, like the TalkTrac Communicator™ fit on the wrist like a wristwatch (see image at right). Low-tech devices are popular because they are usually very portable and user-friendly. VOCAs have been successfully used with preschoolers with autism, increasing their communicative interactions (Schepis et al., 1998).

Messages on Wrist VOCA

| I need help | I need a break | bathroom | I'm finished |

The Picture Communication Symbols®, 1981-2005, Mayer-Johnson, LLC. Used with permission. Mayer-Johnson LLC reserves all rights worldwide.

However, all of this hinges on the response a person with ASD has to voice output. Some people with ASD are very attuned to a VOCA while others are overstimulated or perseverate with the device and are less engaged in an activity as a result. These variable responses to voice output can differ among people with ASD and also with the same person at different stages of development. Parents and practitioners can simply try using the VOCA. After several trials, it should be clear whether the person is more engaged and responsive with or without it.

Combining No- and Low-tech AAC

AAC tools can be combined if that provides the most effective approach to addressing the communication needs of a person with ASD. In the following scenario, Annie is using two AAC devices: a single switch VOCA to get the attention of her peers *and* a communication board with the vocabulary she needs to be an active participant in the activity. You might ask "Why doesn't Annie have one large VOCA so that all her messages can be on one device?" There are several reasons for this: first, no-tech communication boards are less expensive and often equally effective, and second, if a student is transitioning to an expensive VOCA with multiple message capability, the no-tech communication boards are a logical in-between step.

Illustration of Combining No- and Low-tech AAC: Annie and her Cooperative Learning Group

Annie is a bright-eyed eight-year-old diagnosed with autism who has been reading since she was two years old. She is nonverbal and rarely engages anyone for play in the neighborhood school she attends. She uses activity specific Natural Aided Language communication boards with words instead of pictures written in each of the cells. She is in a cooperative learning group with five of her classmates and has a "Making Stone Soup" communication board with her for that activity. Her classmates are chattering about what ingredients they want to put in their soup. Annie is pointing to words on her communication board, "Want carrots," "Want potatoes," "Want peas." Unfortunately, none of her peers are noticing that she is contributing to the activity. Finally, Annie touches her single switch AAC voice output device, the Talking Symbols®, and says "Hey, listen, I want to tell you something." Her peers stop, turn towards her, and watch Annie's communication board as she tells them by pointing, "I want to put in carrots, please." (See table below.)

"Making Stone Soup" Communication Bord

Stone Soup	want	cut	carrots	crock pot
I	turn on	taste		hot
	cook	put in	celery	mmm, good
	smell	eat	turnips	
please	Thank you	spoon	peas	finished

High-tech Devices

High-tech AAC are the most complex electronic communication devices. The most simple of the high-tech varieties to use are the voice output devices that have the capability of eight minutes or more of digitized (recorded) speech. Many of these VOCAs have changeable grid formats to accommodate from approximately five to forty-eight different message cells. These VOCAs can use PCS, photos, or other visual symbols. They can be customized with written words for the AAC user with literacy skills.

High-tech VOCAs have multiple "levels" with the capacity for approximately four to ten activity-specific overlays. Corresponding overlays can be manually inserted into the frame enclosing the grid. Levels can be easily changed with a switch so that the AAC user can access different vocabulary for a variety of environments and activities. In some devices, overlay grids can be  changed to accommodate different grid patterns and therefore numbers of message cells. In others, individual caps can be placed on a message cell to limit the vocabulary on the overlay. This allows the AAC device to grow with the user. Parents, practitioners, or communication partners can customize the number of symbols on one overlay from, for example, four for a beginning AAC user, to thirty-two as the user progresses. Overlay grids for many VOCAs can be accessed through the Boardmaker program, allowing parents or practitioners to create communication overlays for specific commercial AAC devices. These multiple level VOCAs are easy to program and use and take standard batteries as well as AC adapters to power them. The downside to some high-tech devices is their expense and the fact that programming them can be difficult for practitioners.

Illustration of High-tech VOCA Application: Michael and Zachary

Michael, who has Pervasive Developmental Disorder-Not Otherwise Specified (PDD-NOS), is an engaging seven-year-old with a "want to please" personality. Michael is non-verbal and communicates through vocalizations and gestures. In spite of this diagnosis, Michael seeks social connections with his sibling and peers.

Michael's family requests an AAC assessment at his IEP meeting. Looking at Michael's communication needs through the Social Networks (Blackstone & Berg, 2004) AAC assessment (see chapter 4) his family identifies after-school time and Saturdays as times when Michael most needs a way to interact and communicate with his family, in particular his brother Zachary. His family decides that a structured game activity using a multi-level VOCA is something both Michael and Zachary will enjoy. (See figure below.) It will provide lots of opportunities for family togetherness and communication. Michael's family identifies what vocabulary and phrases to include by taking an inventory of Zachary's language when he plays Go Fish with his dad. Michael's mom and dad play with the two boys and model the use of the VOCA. They pair what they say with activating the VOCA. All communication partners are using the VOCA; Michael for expressive language, and Zachary, Mom, and Dad, to augment their speech. As Michael's communication partner, Zachary learns to interact with Michael using the VOCA.

"Go Fish" Overlay for Level One of Multi-Level VOCA

Note that some of the cells on the communication board are empty, with no vocabulary. This is acceptable and appropriate. As the family engages in this activity, they may discover that additional vocabulary is needed. As in all AAC interventions, the language and vocabulary are dynamic and need to be changed as the needs of the communication partners change.

After a few successes with the Go Fish activity, the family wants to consider other activities that can be engineered communicatively for Michael. This high-tech VOCA has the capacity for twelve levels of communication overlays. The family decides to target a family ritual, their Friday night pizza making activity. The communication overlay below contains all the vocabulary needed for Michael to actively participate and communicate with his family. By replacing the overlay and flipping a switch, Michael or one of his family members can cue up the communication tools for a new activity on this multi-level VOCA.

"Making Pizza" Overlay for Level Two of Multi-Level VOCA

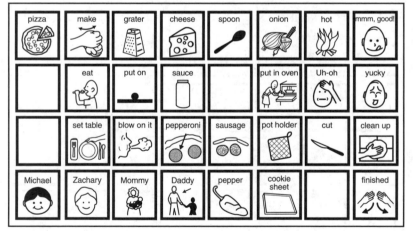

VOCAs with Digitized vs. Synthesized Speech

Some VOCAs use digitized (recorded) speech. While it is acceptable and convenient to record the messages using an adult voice, it is far more natural if the recorded voice is most like that of the non-speaking user in gender and age. Some parents and practitioners will select a peer who is not in the class or family so that the AAC user and her communication partners will identify the voice as more uniquely that of the AAC user and not someone else's.

There are also VOCAs that produce synthesized speech. Practitioners report that some of their students with ASD prefer the sound of synthesized speech because it has a consistent intonation that is somewhat robotic sounding. VOCAs can be programmed to elicit almost unlimited synthesized vocabulary and some of the high-tech devices give the user the option of selecting a synthesized voice that sounds most like the non-speaking communicator in terms of age and gender. These VOCAs are often available with pre-programmed pages and on-screen keyboards.

Dynamic Display Devices

The AAC devices mentioned so far have fixed symbols or written words on communication boards or on voice output devices. The symbols change only when they are actually manually removed and replaced by other sets of symbols. The digitized voice output is changed by manually turning a dial or moving a lever to the desired level. Dynamic display devices have the capability of changing symbol sets and the corresponding speech *electronically* when the AAC user selects a specific symbol. Dynamic display devices have touch sensitive screens that electronically change when the user touches a specific symbol. For example, an electronic "page" on a dynamic display device may display six icons. Each icon represents a particular activity such as lunch, science, social conversation, doing homework, and visiting a friend. When

the AAC user touches the icon for "lunch," the screen changes and shows all the vocabulary needed to communicate and participate in lunch. Dynamic display devices require fewer symbols on each electronic "page" and for some students, fewer symbols enable more accurate selections while providing access to a large vocabulary (Mizuko, Reichle, Ratcliff & Easer, 1994).

Dynamic display devices are dedicated devices (made only as a VOCA) or are programs that can be used with either Macintosh or Windows. They can have both digitized and synthesized speech output, with a choice of voices for the synthesized speech component. Others have on-screen keyboards with text-to-speech capability. For example, if an AAC user types: "I'd like water, please," the device will "speak" that message. Some devices have shortcut keys that can be programmed to generate commonly used messages with one keystroke. These devices also come with preprogrammed pages so that the AAC partners can begin communicating immediately. There are dynamic display devices as small as pocket PCs (ChatPC™) with a bank of five thousand full color PCS symbols. Dynamic display devices are powered by 7V or lithium-ion batteries and plug-in chargers.

Illustration of Transitioning from No-tech to Low-tech to High-tech: Amber and Mr. David

Amber, who has ASD, is a fully included middle school student with an assistant, Mr. David. Amber is interested in science but is not able to fully participate in class. If she knows the answer to a question, she points to the symbol in her communication notebook so her assistant can see it. Mr. David must get the attention of Amber's teacher. Amber is not able to interact directly with her teacher or her peers unless they are right next to her. Mr. David keeps a record of the number of spontaneous communications Amber elicits in class. She averages between one and two per class period with her communication notebook.

After observing her in school, Amber's parents are determined to get their daughter more engaged in learning and interactive with her peers. They request an IEP meeting for the purpose of discussing Amber's AAC system. Amber's speech pathologist, who has expertise in AAC, uses the meeting to do a Social Networks (Blackstone & Berg, 2004) AAC assessment. (Refer to chapter 4 for specifics on this type of assessment.) She particularly focuses on the circle of communication partners that include Amber's peers and general education teachers.

Since Amber can locate specific language boards in her communication binder, the speech pathologist knows Amber understands categories and suggests trying a dynamic display device with voice output. First, the team needs to see if Amber likes voice output, so they give her a VOCA with thirty-two cells and four different levels. Mr. David programs each of the four levels using the vocabulary from her no-tech communication boards. Mr. David uses the VOCA himself interactively and conversationally to model it for Amber.

Finally, Amber is able to communicate directly with her teachers and peers. When she touches the cell for "Hi, what's up?" her classmates respond to her. Amber changes the VOCA to the science vocabulary level and Mr. David puts in the thirty-two cell science overlay. Now, when her teacher asks a question, Amber is able to raise her hand and answer directly with her VOCA. Mr. David notes that her communicative initiations have increased from one or two per class period to three or four.

Since Amber is successful with the VOCA, she is given a dynamic display device. From an initial menu page, (next page, top figure) Amber can touch the science icon and the science vocabulary appears electronically. This VOCA also has a small keyboard that enables her to spell a word that doesn't appear on her screen. Now when Amber wants to answer a question in class, she simply raises her hand and responds using her dynamic display device. Later, during lunch, she switches to her "social" screen (next page, bottom figure) where she has the vocabulary to interact with her peers. Amber no longer needs Mr. David to act as her translator!

Requirements for Successfully Using Dynamic Display Devices

Unlike many no- and low-tech AAC, there are some cognitive prerequisites for the potential high-tech AAC user. A dynamic

Dynamic Display Menu

Let's Talk Overlay

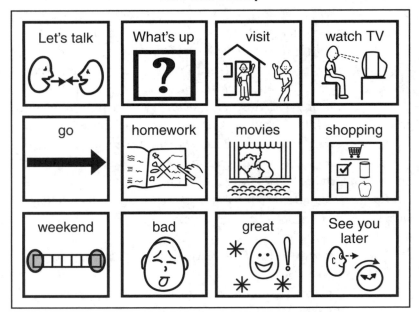

display device requires that the user understand the following:
1. The organization of the vocabulary;
2. that there are other symbols that are not immediately visible but are also available; and
3. the correct selection sequences to access the vocabulary needed (Reichle, Dettling, Drager & Lieter, 2000).

An individual with ASD needs to be able to understand functional categories to be successful with a dynamic display device. Nevertheless, in the case of a potential AAC user with emerging skills in this area, it is always better to assume that the user *has* the potential to learn how to use the device. Always keep in mind that in AAC, the process of experiencing the device as communication often develops latent communication skills.

Pros and Cons of Dynamic Display Devices

Dynamic display devices have strong pros and cons. On the plus side, many dynamic display devices are as small as a hand-held computer, very portable, and don't require physical overlays. Some come with an extensive vocabulary already entered. Parents and practitioners can also customize the vocabulary selections to best meet the needs of the AAC user.

On the negative side, they are very costly. Some are heavy and cumbersome. Their level of sophistication demands more skills from the parents and practitioners programming it. There also may be a learning period that is cognitively labor intensive for the communication partner with ASD. During this time it is imperative that the existing AAC remain in place while skill with the dynamic display is emerging.

Practitioners and parents must understand that the most positive aspect of dynamic display devices—their extensive capability for communication—must outweigh the negative aspects, i.e. the time involved in teaching the staff to program the device, the cost of the device, and the time and energy to maintain it. Keep in mind that there are many people with ASD who have successfully made the transition from multiple language boards to dynamic display devices. In general, an individual can be successful with a dynamic display device when she has communicated by locating and using multiple low-tech communication boards effectively and has shown an acceptance of voice output.

Keyboards as AAC Devices

A keyboard can serve as an AAC device. Keyboards can be as simple as a no-tech alphabet board with letters arranged either alphabetically or in traditional QWERTY format. With an alphabet board, the speaking communication partner provides visual input through pointing to letters to spell out words paired with verbally expressing the words. The non-speaking communication partner points to letters and communicates by spelling. Using an actual keyboard, either with or without voice output, both communication partners type to communicate. Research has shown that when words are typed by both communication partners, people with autism respond (through typing) in longer, more complex sentences (Forsey, Bedrosian & Raining-Bird, 1996).

Illustration of Application of Keyboarding: Kai & Uncle Coleman

Kai is whining and pacing throughout the house. His home routine has been upset by the holidays. Unfamiliar people have been knocking on the door. There are new smells from new foods cooking in the kitchen. Furniture has been rearranged to make room for a six-foot evergreen tree. His continuous whining is a sign that Kai is gearing up for a major tantrum. Since Kai is now twelve years old and almost 120 pounds, his tantrums can be dangerous to himself, family members, and the household.

Kai's Uncle Coleman grabs the AlphaSmart™, a portable word processor, and says as he types, "Kai, what's wrong?" Uncle Coleman pairs his speech with typed language because Kai is not able to understand spoken language and needs the visual component. Kai stops his pacing, looks at the keyboard display and responds by typing, "Want computer. No tree." Uncle Coleman realizes that the computer desk has been moved to make room for the Christmas tree. Uncle Coleman types and says, "Do you want the computer in the front room or the basement?" Kai looks at the keyboard display and types, "basement." His whining stopped, Kai and Uncle Coleman carefully move the computer to a quiet spot in the basement. Kai happily retreats downstairs to work on his computer.

It is, of course, easiest to engage in keyboard conversations when the communication partners have some basic literacy skills. However, seemingly illiterate people with ASD have *developed* literacy-based communication skills from continued opportunities receiving symbol and keyboard-based communicative input from their partners. Anecdotally, many practitioners report that there are children with ASD as young as three years old with the literacy skills that enable them to give and receive communication through simple keyboard spelling.

Keyboard Advantages

Some keyboard AAC devices have the capability of programming specific keys for commonly used messages. In this way, with one keystroke, the AAC user can generate one message. For example, a keyboard AAC user can press only one key to say, "Hi, what's up?" Some high-tech VOCAS have the capability for keyboard communication, as seen in the story of Amber above. In this way, the AAC user is able to spell words that may not already be on the dynamic display device.

Other keyboard devices with displays, such as small electronic hand-held spellers, can serve as AAC tools by providing visual communicative input and generating communicative output. These devices are used conventionally as dictionaries and spelling tools but can function quite well as a keyboard AAC tool. These spelling tools have a small display screen, they are inexpensive, and quite effective for some people with ASD.

Keyboards with a larger area to display typed communication can be even more useful. The AlphaSmart, for example, is a

small, electronic, battery operated, full sized keyboard with an LCD display. It is more costly than the smaller electronic spellers. The display on the AlphaSmart for typed communication is six inches long and one inch wide. This display can show four lines of typed text at once. This enables the person with ASD to view the message she types as well as the message she receives from her communication partner. Once typed, the message remains on the LCD display, providing the static, non-transient visual input that is much easier to process and use for people with ASD.

Keyboard Devices with Voice Output

There are more costly and sophisticated keyboard devices that have the capability for voice output, including some picture-based VOCAs with keyboarding capabilities, and dynamic display devices with on-screen keyboards. These devices require users to type their communicative message and press a "read" or "return" key that will then speak the message. Some of these devices display the typed communication so that the communication partners can both see and hear the message. This is particularly helpful for individuals with ASD since the message remains fixed for the period of time necessary for her to process it. In addition, some voice output keyboard devices have the option of an ABC or QWERTY arrangement. Other options include spell-checking and word prediction. Word prediction increases the speed and ease of typed communication. As the user types the beginning letters of a word, the device anticipates or "guesses" which word the user is looking for, allowing her to simply select the correct word. This is particularly helpful for individuals with ASD who are beginning readers and spellers. For some people with ASD, a voice output keyboard, as with other voice output devices, has two advantages: 1) it can summon the attention of the communication partner, and 2) it can be a model for spoken language. Sometimes these more sophisticated communication devices provide an element of interest, status, and prestige among the peers of the person using it.

What about Facilitated Communication (FC)?

Facilitated Communication (FC) is a method of providing support to individuals with severe communication challenges as they convey typed messages (National Academy of Science, 2001). It is a teaching strategy for keyboard or picture communication and not a method of communication in itself. Facilitated Communication was very popular in the previous decade, but today it is controversial.

Who Facilitated Communication, the supports given are physical, communicative, and emotional. The physical support is given by a facilitator, who is often but not always, the communication partner for the non-speaking individual. The supports vary from providing stability to the typing hand by anchoring the wrist or forearm, isolating the typing finger from the hand, or just providing tactile support on an arm or shoulder. Emotional support consists of encouragement and acknowledgement of all communicative attempts. In studies, it was found that the facilitators—not the people with ASD—were the authors of the typed messages. There is a lack of scientific evidence in tightly controlled studies validating Facilitated Communication.

This lack of quantitative evidence to support Facilitated Communication should not in any way discourage parents and practitioners from considering keyboards as communication options, nor should opportunities to provide literacy instruction be ignored. There are qualitative studies of individuals with ASD who participated in Facilitated Communication and are now independent typing communicators. Providing physical support in keyboarding must involve a systematic fading of those prompts and physical supports with the ultimate goal of encouraging functional, spontaneous, unprompted communication.

Iconic Coding Devices

Iconic coding devices have the most communicative potential but are the most sophisticated, costly, and difficult to use forms of AAC. MinSpeak™ (Baker, 1986) is an iconic coding system. To date, these devices have been effective with only a very few individuals with ASD. Iconic coding devices use picture symbol sequences to generate messages. These devices reduce the number of keystrokes needed to communicate and therefore accelerate the communication process. In other words, symbol combinations are coded and there is no one-to-one correspondence between the symbol and message. For example, to say the word "walk," the user would touch the picture of a "shoe" and the word "verb." This communication code is based on specific rules that often involve understanding abstract concepts. Of course, it is known that many individuals with ASD have great difficulty with abstract concepts. Nonetheless, there are a few reports of people with ASD who have learned to use iconic coding devices. AAC for individuals with autism is a very new field and research on iconic coding is almost nonexistent. Even practical information is quite limited. Perhaps in the near future, there will be methods of determining which people with ASD can most effectively learn to use iconic coding devices.

WordPower™ and Picture WordPower™ (Inman, 2004)

Two new aided AAC systems worth mentioning are WordPower and Picture WordPower (Inman, 2004). WordPower is a word-based

Word Power

HOW	WHAT	qu	w	e	r	t	y	u	i	o	p	PLEASE	THANK YOU	DAY	NOW	TIME
WHEN	WHERE	a	s	d	f	g	h	j	k			delete	BAD	GOOD	TODAY	TOMOR ROW	YESTER DAY
WHO	WHY	space	z	x	c	v	b	n	m	.	?	COLD	HOT	BAG	BATH ROOM	BED
I	ME	MY	TO	BE	CALL	CHANGE	COME	A	ANY	EVERY	SOME	MORE	MUCH	CAR	CHAIR	MEDI CINE
IT	WE	AM	ARE	DRINK	EAT	FEEL	FIND	ALL	ABOUT	AND	AT	OKAY	TIRED	PAIN	PIL LOW	TV
HE	HIM	CAN	COULD	GET	GIVE	GO	HELP	THAT	BE CAUSE	BUT	BY	REALLY	VERY	1	2	3
SHE	HER	DID	DO	HURT	KNOW	LIKE	LOVE	THE	DOWN	FOR	FROM	FOR WARD	BACK	4	5	6
THEY	THEM	HAD	HAS	MAKE	MOVE	NEED	PUT	THIS	HERE	IF	IN	LEFT	RIGHT	7	8	9
YOU	YOUR	HAVE	IS	RUB	SAY	SCRATCH	TAKE	-ed	OF	OFF	ON	SUN	UNCOM FORT ABLE	$	0	:
DON'T	NOT	WAS	WERE	TALK	TELL	THINK	USE	-ing	OR	OUT	OVER	MON	TUES	WED	:00	:15
CAN'T	WON'T	WILL	WOULD	WALK	WANT	WATCH	WORK	-s	THERE	UP	WITH	THUR	FRI	SAT	:30	:45
Ask me yes/no questions	YES															NO

software package and Picture WordPower (shown below) is a picture-based one that can be used as no-tech AAC or with electronic voice output communication aids (VOCA). WordPower uses a core vocabulary of one hundred of the most commonly spoken words. It is used by AAC users with some literacy skills. It is easy to use and requires a minimum of training for communication partners. Currently, it is the hottest program in AAC.

Things to Consider When Selecting AAC Tools and Devices for an Intervention

It is important to provide every person with ASD or communication challenges opportunities with AAC, however, the process of matching a particular AAC tool or strategy with a particular person can be a complex and sometimes "thorny" process. Individuals with ASD often have uneven patterns of development: bursts of skill acquisition, plateaus, and sometimes periods of regression. Thus, it is difficult to pigeonhole a person with ASD into a particular stage of communication development and make decisions about what is and is not an appropriate intervention.

Picture WordPower

Photo courtesy of Prentke Romich Company. www.prentrom.com

The process is made more complex due to the wide variety of AAC tools and strategies available. It is important for practitioners and parents to understand that non-speaking communication partners and speaking communication partners use multiple communication tools similarly. Speaking communication partners use speech, gestures, and body language—all forms of unaided communication only requiring the use of their bodies. They also use hand- or type written letters, cell phones, and e-mails to communicate, all examples of communication aided by tools. Likewise, people with autism use many communication modalities: vocalizations, speech, manual signs, communication boards, voice output devices, alphabet boards, and e-mail. AAC is meant to enhance any existing functional language, not replace it, whether this communication is in the form of manual sign, gestures, vocalizations, or limited speech.

People with ASD can employ a variety of AAC systems, using the most appropriate and available for any given moment. For example, a person may use manual signs with family members and a communication board with teachers and peers. There is no "cookie cutter" approach to AAC interventions. Each tool is selected for a particular time in a person's life and is meant to be changed, adapted, or adjusted as needed.

Many school systems have assistive technology (AT) teams that conduct assessments and make specific AAC recommendations. Clearly, there is a range of AAC tools and devices from simple to complex and AAC specialists may recommend any one of a variety of AAC tools, from communication boards to voice output devices. Recommendations are made based on what is most appropriate for the child at that time. A no-tech or low-tech tool is often the best way to start a child using AAC. While limited speakers with ASD who are cognitively more able *may* be successful with a more complex device, sophisticated voice output devices are generally recommended after a child has demonstrated understanding of the symbols or letters used in no- and low-tech AAC. The technology team can then provide a higher tech device on a trial basis. When this is done, the child's communication progress should be carefully monitored.

Despite these general recommendations, there are no hard rules or clear sequences for trying out AAC tools and strategies. You would not, for example, *necessarily* first use Picture Exchange Communication System (PECS), then proceed to interactive aided language communication boards, and then to voice output. There are instances when parents and practitioners may select a particular

combination of no-tech, low-tech, and high-tech AAC as part of a single intervention, because it is the most effective way of supporting communication. Some AAC users with autism are able to select the most convenient AAC tool for a particular situation themselves. It is important for parents and practitioners to be flexible, then, in supporting multi-modal communication when that is most appropriate. And having your child assessed by a qualified AAC specialist or assistive technology team is always your best approach to matching up your unique child or student with the right intervention tools.

There are many significant factors that may affect the type of device selected by your child's IEP team, some of which are clearly outside the isolated needs of the potential AAC user. Listed below are aspects and features your intervention team should take into consideration when selecting AAC tools and strategies for your child or student.

Selecting a Symbol System

When choosing between using the available symbol systems, i.e. tangible vs. representational vs. written words vs. some combination for your child or student with AAC, consider the following. How strong a visual processor is your child? How engaged is your child with print? This will give you an indication of how likely she is to respond to a specific system. The process of determining an initial course of action may be largely trial and error. Sometimes your child will require repeated long-term exposure to a system before you see a response, so be patient.

Ease of Use for Programmers

AAC specialists and trainers often report that if practitioners and parents find that a device is not "user-friendly," meaning it is too difficult to program or use, it will not be used and the AAC user will not have access to any communication system. Regardless of the communicative potential of the new AAC user, it is the communication partners who select the vocabulary and program the device, so ease of use and programmability is often a defining factor in a successful AAC intervention.

Ease of Use for the AAC User

For the AAC user with ASD, learning to use AAC is a process and this process provides the stimulus for developing language. A first AAC tool will most likely be a no-tech communication board because the technology is universally understood and practitioners can implement it easily. No-tech AAC interventions also provide useful information on the processing ability of the user. Sometimes a potential AAC user will be more engaged and more communicative with a VOCA. It is unlikely a first-time AAC user will be given a high-tech device since the assessment process usually involves trials with low- or no-tech, with recommendations for high-tech only after the student has shown proficiency with lower tech tools.

Type of Speech Output

Often students with ASD will have had the opportunity to use AAC devices as part of their classroom instruction. Information from classroom practitioners as to how a student responds to a particular type of voice output can guide in the selection of a device for that student. School-based AAC teams can provide devices on a trial basis to determine a student's response to the type of voice output. (Keep in mind, however, that the type of speech output is often not the primary consideration in selecting AAC.) Some people with ASD prefer a synthesized voice since it is more consistent in sound, inflection, and intonation than the digitized speech and therefore easier to understand. These devices will also have a variety of synthesized voices to best match the age and gender of the AAC user. Digitized speech is more natural sounding since it is an actual recorded voice. It is important to select a person close in age and gender to record the messages on digitized AAC devices so it sounds most natural. Parents and practitioners need to observe the AAC user's response to the speech output to insure that the AAC user grows to recognize that voice as her own.

Cost

Cost is another factor that must realistically be considered. School systems are required to provide an AAC device if it enables a student to access the curriculum, the IEP, and participate in a less restrictive environment. School systems are not required to purchase the most expensive device if two different devices provide similar benefit. Parents or caregivers may also want to purchase an AAC device in addition to the one provided by their school system. No- and low-tech tools and devices can be made or purchased very inexpensively. They generally range in price from free to $500. The high-tech multiple level devices described above range in price from slightly over $100 to $1200. Others, not described in this primer, are significantly more expensive.

Portability and Durability

Portability is also an important consideration. Communication opportunities are everywhere and AAC should be convenient and easy to carry. No- and low-tech devices can be fairly easy to transport, (e.g., communication wallets), though are sometimes cumbersome, (e.g., thick three-ring binders). Fortunately, unlike some types of high-tech devices, they are easily replaced if necessary. Some multiple level VOCAs come with built in handles; others come with a carrying case or shoulder strap. There are multiple-level VOCAs that are the size of a hand-held computer (like a palm pilot). The weight range for these devices ranges from about seven ounces to two and a half pounds. In terms of durability, some of these devices have cases with a moisture guard; others come with durable housing that can withstand physical trauma.

Setting Up AAC for Success

To get geared-up to implement an AAC intervention for your child or student, keep in mind these keys to success. In fact, make a copy of this list and post it in your classroom or on your refrigerator at home.

- **Assume that the person with ASD *can* communicate.** Assume that she is cognitively more able than she appears. This will qualitatively change your approach.
- **Engineer the environment for communication and participation** by using standard best practices in autism methodologies and reputable AAC strategies, such as visual schedules, visual cueing tools, Natural Aided Language, incidental teaching, etc.
- **Create opportunities for communication.** Make desired things, such as food, toys, and reinforcers visible but not accessible so that the AAC user has to use her AAC tool or device to ask for them. Use creative sabotage by stopping a routine or familiar activity and provide vocabulary on an AAC tool so that the AAC user can request that you resume. For example, unplug the DVD player so that when the person with ASD puts in the DVD and turns it on, nothing happens. Be sure to have the vocabulary available for the child to say, "Please help me," or "Plug it in," or "The DVD player is broken."
- **Choose a motivating, reinforcing activity or environment for your first AAC intervention.**

- **Assess the environment or activity.** Is it appropriately stimulating; neither too boring nor too difficult?
- **Select initial AAC tools that are easy** for parents, practitioners, and the person with autism to use, such as no-tech communication boards and low-tech VOCAs.
- **Select rich vocabulary** that includes nouns, verbs, and descriptors. Even for a developmentally young person with ASD, a simple communication board with eight symbols can provide a rich language experience. Rather than starting with too simple an intervention, it is often better to "raise the bar" first in terms of the vocabulary selected. The practitioner can always decrease the amount and level of vocabulary provided if need be. Be sure to include vocabulary that enables communication partners to question, respond, and comment, even when the non-speaking partner has not shown signs of being able to do so. Parents and practitioners must use their best instincts, educated guesses, as well as concrete information about the potential AAC user in selecting vocabulary and messages for the AAC tool.
- **Be sure that the device has all the vocabulary needed for the AAC user to be actively involved.**
- **Include more vocabulary words than the user actually knows.** These will be the stimulus for learning new words and new concepts and ultimately developing more complex language.
- **Give the AAC user time to explore or practice with a new device.** Provide sufficient supervision for safety but refrain from trying to control their practicing.
- **View AAC as a second language** adopted into your environment.
- **Use the AAC device!** Speaking communication partners should acknowledge that this is a real language by using the tool or device; augmenting their own speech and therefore modeling its use.

- **Keep providing input.** Remember that communication is expressive and receptive. If your communication partner with autism is responding to AAC by making eye contact with visual symbols, following visual directions, or managing behavior with visual cues, that is a sign of success. Expressive language will eventually emerge.

- **Make certain AAC is convenient and available** to every user, because, of course, it is their voice! For aided AAC tools and devices, (since unaided AAC, i.e. manual signs, vocalizations, and gestures are part of a person's body), there is an assortment of commercial and homemade gear that keeps the AAC with the user. These include shoulder straps, key chains, belt loops, and fanny packs. These keep the AAC device where it belongs: with the AAC user.

- **Give it time.** It is important for all practitioners to remember that learning to use an AAC tool or device and adopting it as one's own voice takes time. Some people with autism learn to understand visual language immediately; others take months and even years.

Insuring Your Child Receives Maximum Benefit from Her AAC Tool or Device

The ability to generate functional spontaneous communication is the most critical skill for people with autism to learn. Parents and practitioners, as the child's primary communication partners, must work as a team to insure seamless coverage across all environments. Training and ongoing support in programming, using, and maintaining the AAC device should be available to each of your child's communication partners. This is most commonly where an AAC intervention breaks down. When parents, caregivers, and teachers don't receive adequate training to use the AAC tools, often they use them inappropriately, don't use them consistently, or don't implement them at all. Working together will help you avoid these pitfalls. Parents, caregivers, and practitioners can do the following to support one another and insure that their child or student will make the most progress engaging in interactive functional communication:

1. Parents should be an integral part of the development of an AAC intervention, including identifying communication environments and communication partners, selecting AAC tools, and choosing vocabulary and specific language stimulation strategies.

2. Parents and caregivers should insure that the AAC tool or device is sent home each day so that communication at home and in school is mutually reinforcing. This should be written into the notes in the child's IEP.

3. Parents, caregivers, and practitioners should communicate daily or at the very least several times a week to share information about how AAC is being used in each setting, which communication strategies are most effective, and who the current communication partners are.

4. As a parent and your child's primary home communication partner, it's crucial that you use the AAC device consistently at home and send it back to school each weekday.

5. Parents can be active partners with their child's practitioner to insure the AAC device is properly maintained by keeping it clean, dry, protected from potential damage, charged, and filled with fresh batteries.

6. Parents have the right to expect that the AAC tool or device is readily accessible to their child while in school. AAC tools and devices should never be in closets, cabinets or lockers.

7. A parent can request an IEP meeting at any time if she believes that the AAC tool or strategy is not appropriate or needs updating. The child's school is required to comply with such a request.

Troubleshooting

Stimming or Playing with a Voice Output Device— Is It Practicing or Perseverating?

Voice output, whether on a keyboard or a picture-based AAC device has its unique challenges. Some individuals with ASD find that striking the same key over and over is more interesting to them than actually communicating with a device. There's no doubt that using it in this way can be extremely annoying to parents and practitioners, not to mention other potential communication partners in the environment. Some VOCAs have keyboard adjustments that minimize or even prevent a message or key being played over and over.

If you have a student who seems to be perseverating on a particular word or phrase, she is probably enjoying the experience! Some practitioners feel that when an AAC device or new vocabulary is introduced, an individual may want explore the device or the new vocabulary. In this case, I would tend to give the user the benefit of the doubt and not remove the device just because of the perseveration. This *may* be a form of practicing with the AAC device. Parents and practitioners should consider providing a daily "practice period" for their new AAC VOCA users for just that purpose.

It's important to be certain the activity you're asking your student to participate in is appropriately engaging. If the perseverating behavior continues, perhaps she's simply not sufficiently stimulated. However, if it appears that the device is being used for solitary amusement and not for communication or if the voice output component is distracting or disturbing to the AAC user, action should be taken. In my experience, dealing with this behavior is best handled by calling an IEP meeting to discuss alternatives to the voice output device. It may be necessary to replace the device with no-tech communication boards and try voice output again in six months. Communication partners would then continue to provide communicative input by augmenting their spoken communication with visual symbols, i.e. pictures or words on the communication boards.

Others argue that if a stereotypic or perseverative behavior is persistent or intrusive, it is important to do a functional behavior assessment (FBA) to determine what factors are related to the behavior. Based on the results, practitioners develop interventions to target that behavior. For example, if a behavior appears to have an "automatic" or inherently reinforcing quality, they might use a brief ten to fifteen second "quiet hands" procedure during which the child places her hands on the table or in her lap, before the device is returned to her. If the assessment suggests the student does not yet understand how to use the equipment appropriately, the intervention might involve providing a simpler form of AAC.

Commonly Asked Questions

We did an assessment and provided a device but my child just isn't using it!

The first question to ask is: Are her communication partners using the device? In other words, is your child receiving receptive language input with the AAC? If she is looking at the symbols and attending to the input, then she is receiving language and the device is effective. Expressive language will follow; just be patient and keep providing receptive language input.

My student used to use his device very effectively and now no longer wants anything to do with it. What can I do?

Are the environments within which you are using the device reinforcing? Does the student have opportunities for hands-on engagement in the activity? The student may have become tired or bored with the activity. Identify other activities or environments that may be more motivating. Add more vocabulary and keep providing input. Developmental or medication changes may also affect AAC use. Take these into consideration. Try using a simpler AAC method to provide a bridge over this difficult period.

My student wants to use my hand and finger to point to the symbols on his AAC device. What can I do?

This is a common occurrence when the introduction of the AAC tool includes physical prompting. Many people with ASD will link physical contact with their communication partner's hand with communicating. Break this habit by avoiding hand-over-hand support and gently separating your hands from each other. Instead, give receptive language input by pointing to symbols while you are talking to her.

School professionals tell me that my child is too low-functioning for AAC. What can I do?

First, most AAC interventions require no prerequisite skills. Some high-tech devices and methods, like dynamic display devices and keyboarding, require some basic skills, but most no- and low-tech techniques are perfectly viable early interventions. Second, communication is a basic right for all people. AAC not only provides a means to communicate, it helps *develop* communication. Request an IEP meeting and an AAC assessment. In the meantime, give your child visual input when communicating with her. Use visual schedules and activity schedules to help her negotiate her routines.

I am afraid that if we use visual symbols with my child she may never learn to talk.

This is a common concern for parents and practitioners. There is no research demonstrating that AAC inhibits speech. In fact, existing research, although limited, has found that AAC stimulates speech. AAC is also never a substitute for existing speech, but a way to enhance it. In addition, Natural Aided Language provides consistent, repetitive language stimulation in motivating contexts. It is simply carrying out standard best practices in teaching language to people with autism.

My child has the same diagnosis and seems to share many of the same skills and deficits as one of his classmates who is very successful using a high-tech

VOCA. Should we start our son with this device right off the bat?

It is very important to select a device that is most appropriate for your child. Autism is a "spectrum" disorder, so regardless of similarities between people with ASD, they are all quite different from one another. It is always best to begin with a simple no- or low-tech tool to determine how well your child can discriminate between various symbols and access the tool or device for real communication. School systems are usually quite reluctant to purchase an expensive device without first finding out whether that is the best option for the student. A school AAC team may provide a particular VOCA on a trial basis to determine its suitability for that student. A device that is too difficult to use can potentially "turn-off" the student to AAC entirely. For students who can access funding for a device through Medicaid, there may be limitations on how often that funding source can be used. In cases such as this, if you purchase a device that is not appropriate, you will not be able to purchase a more appropriate one—even if it is less expensive—for a period of several years.

I have a student who is very destructive. I don't want to give her an AAC device for fear that she will destroy it or use it to hurt herself or others.

Difficult behaviors are never a reason not to provide AAC for people with ASD. In fact, your student's inability to communicate may be the very reason she is engaging in destructive behavior. Use no-tech communication boards and communication wallets first. Try laminating the communication boards with heavy-duty laminate for greater durability.

I have a child who uses a portable keyboard to communicate and he is beginning to use speech. Is it time to take away the AAC to encourage more spontaneous speech?

This is a good question and one that is difficult to answer. To date, there is no research showing that removing a familiar AAC device will either stimulate or discourage more speech. Speech, of course, is the most portable, convenient, and universally used method of communication and functional spontaneous speech is an appropriate goal for people with ASD. Limited research and practitioner reports indicate that people with ASD will comprehend more visual than auditory language, will generate more language with AAC than with their own voice, and will accept unanticipated changes when they are presented visually.

A parent or practitioner may decide to use AAC to introduce and establish more complex language and encourage the use of speech in more simple routine activities. It is important to consider, however, that if speech is generated in response to a verbal prompt, fading that prompt will require planning. Finally, it is extremely important to honor an individual's functional communication system. Removing AAC devices that have become a person's real voice and ears should be done with extreme caution and sensitivity.

I am giving my student receptive language input and she is not responding. In fact, she looks away. How long should I continue?

If you have been providing intensive visual language input and the person with ASD is neither looking at the symbols nor showing any response to them, it may be time to try a different symbol system, such as concrete, tangible symbols or photographs. In addition, make certain you are introducing the symbol system in a highly reinforcing context. Identify more motivators and build communication around those items or activities.

It is not unreasonable to provide receptive language input for six months or more before you get a response from the person with ASD. During this time, you are communicating with your child or student in motivating environments and you are providing a consistent and predictable language framework. This alone is beneficial.

If a person with ASD appears to understand augmented input although she is not yet generating any output, then you've achieved some success in receptive language. Looking at the communication board, complying with visual instructions, following visual schedules, or accepting a disappointment when given visually are all indications that the intervention is a success.

4 | AAC Assessments: Identifying Communication Needs and the Tools to Address Them

Finding the right fit, or matching the appropriate AAC device to the user, is a process that is not at all like purchasing a pair of shoes. It is first and foremost a dynamic process that takes time and requires careful observation and assessment. AAC assessment is not a "one-time" event; rather it evolves. Because of the dynamic nature of communication development and the rapid advances in AAC technologies, assessment is always an ongoing process. The goal of any augmentative & alternative communication intervention is to provide the supports that will enable a person to better communicate with others. Therefore, an AAC assessment must take into consideration a person's existing expressive and receptive language; i.e. what he can convey and what he can understand.

An IEP, or Individualized Education Program, is a detailed description of the learning program your child will receive from his school. It includes information on your child's current areas of progress and

need. The IEP team consists of the student himself, his parents, and the practitioners who provide his educational services. The team convenes once a year to review your child's progress and develop goals and objectives for the following school year. Your child's IEP team *must consider* the need for AAC at each and every IEP meeting.

If you, as a parent, or the team believe that your child can benefit from AAC or that a change to his existing AAC system is needed, an assessment will follow to identify the precise tools and strategies required at that point in time. It is important to note that you can request an IEP meeting and an AAC assessment at *any time* and the school is required to comply. There is a timeframe mandated by law that defines when an AAC assessment should be completed. There should be no more than thirty days from the time a parent requests an evaluation to the completion of the evaluation. Although IDEA (Individuals with Disabilities Education Act) mandates this, states have different interpretations of this regulation. The following website gives up-to-date information on the status of timelines in the newly updated IDEA 2004: www.cec.sped.org. More on the legal aspects of getting an assessment will be covered in chapter 5.

AAC Assessment Tools

Several types of AAC assessments representative of what's available are summarized in this chapter. Those included are considered formal assessments in that they follow a prescribed format and are comprehensive in nature. Informal assessments are more observational in nature although they incorporate elements of more formal ones and can be just as effective. An AAC assessment may be conducted by any practitioner with expertise in AAC, including special educators, speech and language pathologists (SLP), occupational therapists (OT), physical therapists (PT), psychologists, or assistive technology specialists. Some universities and professional organizations offer professional certification and degrees in AAC and assistive technology. At this time, there are no regulations limiting who is qualified to do assessments. Because of the unique processing styles of people with autism, it is crucial that the assessment be conducted by someone with expertise in both AAC *and* ASD.

School-based AAC assessments are always conducted in natural, or "real," as opposed to staged settings and in the environments in which the AAC device or strategy will be used. Information is gathered from the child's classroom teacher, speech and language pathologist, occupational therapist, as well as general and special educators. The child's other communication partners, like peers and siblings, might also provide input for the assessment process. AAC specialists also observe the child in his natural school settings. Sometimes videotaping a child in his natural environment is helpful in guiding the team in the assessment process.

Since the assessment process involves observing the student in his own environment, the student's participation in the assessment is limited to simply interacting with his environment and his potential communication partners. According to IDEA (Individuals with Disabilities Education Act) regulations, however, a person with a disability is part of the IEP team and as such can be a participating member in the assessment process as much as he is able.

After the child's parents and practitioners share their observations, the next step involves completing any one of a variety of inventories. There are several existing AAC assessment tools. Three representative ones will be highlighted here. They are the Participation Model (Beukelman & Mirenda, 1998), the SETT Framework (Zabala, 2000), and Social Networks (Blackstone & Berg, 2004). Each of these employ the "environmental" approach, meaning they approach AAC assessment in a naturalistic and ongoing way, considering carefully the realms in which the person with ASD lives and works, the tasks he must perform in those environments, and the communication partners he encounters. A number of school AAC teams develop their own assessments with some of the features of each of the assessments mentioned.

These assessment models operate under the assumption that communication needs change and therefore assessments need to be dynamic, flexible, and ongoing to mirror those changes. This means that at each IEP meeting, whether regularly scheduled or requested by a parent, the effectiveness of the existing AAC is reviewed in light of present and future communication needs. In this way, relevant portions of the assessment can be updated to reflect new communication environments and potential communication opportunities.

The Participation Model *(Beukelman & Mirenda, 1998)*

The Participation Model identifies the communication partners and the communication needs of a person with limited or no speech. This model considers the physical, cognitive, and language skills of a person in order to determine which AAC tool is most appropriate for him. It looks at how the individual communicates and participates at home, school, or in the community in comparison to his typically developing peers. In this way, it is possible to see what is the most age appropriate place, vocabulary, and tool for an initial AAC intervention. This model also looks at the communication barriers and the communication opportunities present in a typical day for the individual. It considers how to create an AAC tool and intervention that will address many environments and situations for the AAC user as he grows and changes (Beukelman & Mirenda, 1998). The goal of this assessment is to develop a working participation plan for the student.

It is essential that progress be measured in an AAC intervention so that appropriate adjustments can be made to insure the child's greatest level of participation in each environment. Some time after the initial assessment happens and the AAC tools and strategies have been put into place, the AT team is responsible for following up with a review of the communication equipment, the skills of the communication partners, and the abilities of the AAC user. A practitioner may use anecdotal records, videotapes, or quantitative measures to guide the ongoing intervention and make needed adjustments. A good resource for AAC data collection is the reader-friendly book, *How Do You Know It? How Can You Show It?* (Reed, Bowser, & Korsten, 2002).

A model of the morning component of a plan developed after an assessment using the Participation Model for a seven-year-old student with autism is shown in Figure 4-1. Notice that each time period of the morning is accounted for.

Figure 4-1

AAC Participation Plan for Andy K.   Jan. 2005

AAC Assessment Team: Mrs. K. (Mom), Mr. K. (Dad), Nick (brother), Ms. Fiore (special educator), Mr. Harris (SLP & AAC specialist), Ms. Curtis (general education teacher)

Environment: Andy's school day

Schedule Activity	Expectations	AAC Adaptations	Support	Evaluation
9-9:15 a.m. Arrival	Put coat & lunch box in locker; Bring home-school communication book to teacher independently	Activity schedule book with PCS	One on one with fading physical prompts	Weekly data: Number of prompts needed to complete routine
9:15-10 c.m. Morning Meeting	Greet teacher & peers	VOCA with recorded greeting "Good morning!"	Teacher modeling use of VOCA with peers at morning meeting	Weekly data: Level of prompt needed to use VOCA
10-10:30 a.m. Reading	Will follow text in reading groups	Text adapted with PCS	Group (three students); Teacher points to PCS on master book	Biweekly Probe data: Time engaged in reading
10:30-11 a.m. Leisure	Will select leisure activity	Choices of preferred activities with PCS on Tech/Talk™ (eight cell VOCA)	Group (students); Teacher asks "What would you like to do?" with fading AAC prompts	Biweekly probe data: Level of prompt needed to select leisure activity
11-11:45 a.m. Lunch with typically developing peers	Will interact with typically developing peers	Placemat communication board with interactive vocabulary	Teacher to teach peer communication partners in Natural Aided Language	Biweekly probe data: Number of initiations using communication board
All day	Ask to use the bathroom	4"x4" "bathroom" PCS mounted with velcro on classroom wall	One on one with fading prompts	Weekly data: Level of prompt needed to give PCS to teacher
All day	Will ask for break	Single switch VOCA with "I need a break" on Andy's desk	One on one with fading AAC prompts	Daily data: Incidence of disruptive behavior and use of VOCA

The SETT Framework: A Collaborative Planning and Decision-Making Tool *(Zabala, 2000)*

SETT is an acronym for Student, Environment, Tasks, and Tools. The SETT framework is actually an assistive technology tool that works well for AAC assessments as well. It is a called a "framework" because it provides the questions and structure that allow the team (e.g., practitioners, parents, speech and language pathologists, psychologists) to identify precisely what a student needs in order to communicate and participate. The goal of the SETT Framework is to help collaborative teams share information and essentially brainstorm within the parameters of the framework. The team is then able to create student-centered, environmentally useful, task-focused assistive technology-based tool systems that facilitate successful participation and communication for people with disabilities (Zabala, 2000). SETT poses the following questions (see Figure 4-2 at right) as stimuli for discussion amongst the team members, who choose one environment and one skill to focus on each time they go to the framework. Following this is a sample result of a brainstorming session—a plan for Keisha, a fourth grader with ASD. (See Figure 4-3 on pages 102-103.)

Figure 4-2

SETT Framework

STUDENT
- What does the individual need to be able to do?
- What are the individual's special needs as related to this task?
- What are the individual's current abilities?
- What are the functional areas of concern?

ENVIRONMENT
- What are the structural and physical arrangements of the environment?
- What supports are available to both student and staff?
- What materials and equipment are currently available?
- What are the physical, instructional, and technological access issues?
- What are the attitudes and expectations of the staff or family?

TASKS
- What specific tasks occur in the individual's natural environment that enable progress towards mastery of IEP goals?
- What specific tasks are required for active involvement in the identified environments, such as communication and participation?

TOOLS

Tools are services, devices, and strategies. Look at the answers to "Student," "Environment," and "Tasks" above to address the following:

1. Will the student not be able to make reasonable progress towards IEP goals without these tools (AAC devices and services)? If "yes," describe a useful system for this individual, including services.
2. Explore other tools that could address participation needs.
3. Select the most appropriate tools for trial use in target environments.
4. Collect data on the effectiveness of the tool.

Figure 4-3

The SETT Framework:
A Collaborative Planning and Decision-Making Tool

<u>Student</u>: Keisha   <u>Date</u>: January 8, 2005

Student	Environment	Tasks	Tools
Needs to do: Participate with peers in leisure activity	Inclusive club period with typically developing peers	What takes place in environment: 1. Peers greet each other 2. Peers arranged in random groups 3. Peers select leisure activity 4. Locate game 5. Distribute game pieces (if necessary) 6. Peers play game (turn taking, commenting, requesting)	No-tech tools: 1. Photos of peers with "Hi" symbol for personally greeting each peer 2. Pencil and paper for keeping score 3. Activity schedule with PCS 4. Game Choice Board with PCS
Special needs: 1. Limited speech 2. Aggressive during transitions	Available materials & equipment: 1. Activity schedule 2. Eight cell VOCA 3. Card & board games	Tasks that address IEP objectives: 1. Greeting peers 2. Selecting leisure activity 3. Matching symbols 4. Turn taking 5. Requesting with AAC 6. Commenting during game 7. Requesting quiet location	Low-tech tools: 1. Nine message Go Talk™ ("My turn," "Your turn," No cheating," "Pick one," "Do you have...," "Uh-oh," "I need to go to the quiet table," "Let's play again," "I won!")
Current Abilities: 1. Emergent literacy 2. Functional speech ("No, want," "Good girl") 3. Chains three symbols to augment speech	Physical arrangement of room: Three circular game tables	Critical elements of task: 1. Interacting with typically developing peers 2. Preempting meltdown by asking for quiet table 3. Making choices	

(Figure 4-3 continued)

Student	Environment	Tasks	Tools
	Special concerns: 1. Noise in room 2. Aggressive behaviors	Keisha will be able to ask to leave the room if noise level becomes too high	"I want to go to the quiet table" on nine message VOCA, the Go Talk™
	Instructional arrangement: Three circular tables with ten typically developing peers & two students with ASD	Modifying game time by: 1. Providing interactive vocabulary on VOCA 2. Teaching peers to pair their speech with visuals 3. Creating "quiet space" within game room 4. Putting PCS on each game choice that will match Keisha's choice board	
	Existing supports in environment: 1. Trained peers 2. One instructional assistant 3. "Quiet table" located at far end of room and sheltered with a room divider	Technology Supports: 1. Visual activity schedules for each component of game time (greeting, grouping, selecting game, playing game, interacting within game, completing game, putting game away) 2. VOCA for interaction 3. VOCA for requesting break	
	Resources available to peers and staff: 1. AAC specialist ½ hour/week 2. School behavior support team		

Social Networks: A Communication Inventory for Individuals with Complex Communication Needs and their Communication Partners
(Blackstone & Berg, 2004)

Social Networks is a comprehensive assessment tool, adapted from Circles of Friends (O'Brien, Forest, Snow, & Hasbury, 1989), that relies on a person's communication partners to identify his potential communication needs and choose appropriate AAC interventions. The first step is to inventory the person's receptive and expressive language, literacy, motor, and adaptive skills, cognition, and any existing technology he uses. Social Networks also considers any other functional communication modes being used such as body language, gestures, vocalizations, speech, even e-mail, and representational strategies such as objects, pictures, symbols, and manual signs. It considers how frequently and effectively these are used by the person being assessed. Social Networks then moves its focus to the communication partners in a person's life.

Social Networks uses the model of concentric circles to differentiate social relationships and potential communication partners of the AAC user. Family members are in the innermost circle, friends are in the next closest circle, followed by acquaintances, paid workers, and unfamiliar partners. Social Networks uses an interview format to gather information from representative persons in each circle as well as from the person with complex communication needs, if this is possible. This tool looks at actual social networks to determine where the potential for communication lies and how AAC supports can address opportunities in those potential areas. This is an essential approach for people with ASD since social interaction is the essential building block for the development of communication.

Figure 4-4 is an example of a Social Networks inventory. The information was gathered by a trained assessor through interviews with Troy's family, friends, and other communication partners. Recommendations for AAC interventions are suggested throughout the report.

Figure 4-4

Sample Social Networks Assessment

Troy is a twelve-year-old boy with ASD. He attends a special program for adolescents with communication disorders in a general education middle school. His parents, peer buddies, and special education and general education teacher meet to conduct an AAC assessment. After completing the first part of the Social Networks inventory, they document that Troy has severe impairment in both receptive and expressive language. He enjoys drawing pictures and describing them with one or two words. He will read literature adapted with PCS. His vision, hearing, and motor skills are within normal range; however, it has been difficult to assess his cognitive ability due to the severity of his language handicap. Troy uses single PCS to request his favorite objects. At home he uses gestures and his family is able to read his body language. He does not have access to any voice output or low-tech communication device either at home or in his classroom.

Troy's primary communication partners at home are his mom and his ten-year-old sister, Jade. Both Mom and Jade are very skilled at understanding and communicating with Troy. At school, Troy spends an equal amount of time with his three teachers, his special education teacher, and the two assistants in class. During specials, such as Art, Music, and PE, Troy has a peer buddy, Luis, who is also skilled at understanding Troy.

In completing the Social Networks inventory, it is determined that in Troy's most intimate (first) circle at home, his primary mode of communication is gestural, but there is a need to expand Troy's communication modes to increase the communication between him and his family. Since Troy has emergent literacy skills, his mom and sister will pair their speech with written words to enhance his receptive language. In addition, a trial use of a keyboard device with voice output will be used both at school and at home. Family members and teachers will give Troy communicative input with this VOCA and keep a log of the initiations and responses Troy makes with his VOCA.

(Figure 4-4 continued)

During his school day, Troy's primary communication partners (second circle) are his teachers and peer buddy, Luis. They will also attempt to increase Troy's communicative interactions by using both PCS, formatted in interactive language boards and handwritten text. The VOCA will also be used in his classroom and during special classes with Troy's friend, Luis.

Troy's third circle, those who support him, such as his bus driver and the workers in the cafeteria, have great difficulty communicating with Troy. They do not understand his gestures and Troy often becomes frustrated when he is not understood. Troy's team creates communication boards with PCS for each of these environments: on the bus and going through the cafeteria line. The team teaches both the bus and cafeteria personnel how Troy will use the board and how they can communicate with him using these tools.

Troy's fourth circle of communication partners includes people he does not see on a regular basis but nonetheless needs to communicate with. Troy will use his communication boards and VOCA. His teacher has programmed the phrase, "You can talk to me by typing" on the VOCA, so that communication partners unfamiliar with Troy (including unfamiliar peers) know how to interact with him.

Troy's fifth circle of communication partners is made up of unfamiliar people Troy may encounter during community training or while out with his family. His communication needs are more limited in this environment while he is living at home because his parents will do much of the communicating for him. In the future, however, Troy will need to know how to communicate with the people within the fifth circle as he takes his place in the community as a young adult. To prepare Troy for this inevitable transition, his VOCA is programmed to help him access the public library independently. Vocabulary for the library consists of conventional niceties such as "Please," "Thank you, "Have a nice day," as well as "Where are the books about horses?"

Commonly Asked Questions

How should we go about choosing an assessment method to use?

The AAC assessments mentioned above, and indeed all good AAC assessments, are environmentally based. That is, they consider the potential AAC user and what he needs to be able to do to participate fully in his environment. Although this chapter mentions specific assessment tools, many school systems and AT teams will use a hybrid assessment that has many of the components of each of the tools. Other AT teams write detailed observations as assessments.

The Participation Plan was developed by two of the "pioneers" in AAC, David Beukelman and Pat Mirenda, and as its title implies, looks at opportunities where communication facilitates participation in the home, school, and community. The SETT Framework is available free on the Internet and provides a user-friendly structure for probing how AAC is inserted into daily activities. Social Networks approaches AAC assessment from the social interaction standpoint, a key area for people with ASD. The Wisconsin Assistive Technology Initiative (WATI) was not detailed in this chapter but is worth mentioning. The WATI is a comprehensive tool that guides the assessment team in considering not only AAC for communication, but also literacy supports. The WATI is also available free on the Internet.

When a team is engaged in the process of obtaining funding for a particular AAC device, a detailed, data-based assessment is usually required. Regardless of which assessment your team uses, it is important that it be comprehensive and take into consideration the often latent communication potential of people with ASD and the potential for AAC to support the development of language.

How can I prepare my child for her assessment, bearing in mind how difficult it can be to get people with ASD to participate in these kinds of things?

There is really nothing a parent or practitioner can do to prepare a person with autism for an assessment. As long as it is a typical day within customary environments and with potential communication partners, the information gleaned will support the development of an appropriate AAC system. If the assessment occurs on an atypical day—say, when the child is having difficulty with a particular activity, for example—that may also signal a place where there is a communication breakdown and highlight where an AAC tool may alleviate those problems.

What about the person conducting the AAC Assessment? What are the elements of a good evaluator?

The individual assessing the person with ASD must have more than simply knowledge of AAC and ASD. What is needed is an open mind and the belief that regardless of difficult behaviors, lack of motivation, or poor demonstration of cognitive ability, every person with autism has the potential to communicate. AAC interventions can stimulate and nurture levels of communication not thought possible.

What are elements of a good evaluation? What should be looked at, uncovered, considered and why?

A good evaluation is above all comprehensive and optimistic. You might say, "How can an evaluation be optimistic?" Evaluators need to view the individual as having the potential to be a communicator. A good evaluation includes recommendations for a consistent and ongoing AAC intervention with frequent receptive language input from communication partners, varying reinforcers, and quantitative data on communication objectives.

What are red flags I should look for that signal the assessor is not looking at the "whole" child? What should you do if you feel important elements are being overlooked?

If, as a parent or practitioner, you feel the assessment accurately measured your child's needs but not his abilities, it is important to address this at an upcoming IEP meeting. Anecdotal records, data, or videotape of your child engaging in an activity that was not demonstrated during the assessment is helpful. For example, while not addressed in the assessment, you have noticed that your child is interested in print and seems to read books or catalogs. This indicates your child has emergent or perhaps developed literacy skills that can be tapped for both receptive and expressive language. In this case, you may advocate for a low- or high-tech keyboard as the primary AAC tool.

Is there some central resource I can go to with questions I have about the assessment process?

There are many electronic resources for assistive technology and AAC services. The Quality Indicators for Assistive Technology Services, or QIAT (http://www.qiat.org) was developed by a team of innovative, forward looking assistive technology specialists. The QIAT is an excellent resource for parents, professionals, school systems, government agencies, and professional organizations. The QIAT addresses the administrative support needed, the role of the IEP team, implementation practices, evaluation, and the role of assistive technology in the transition procedure.

5 | AAC & the Law

Disability is a natural part of the human experience that does not diminish the right of individuals with developmental disabilities to live independently, to exert control and choice over their own lives, and to fully participate in and contribute to their communities through full integration and inclusion in the economic, political, social, cultural, and educational mainstream of United States society.

—*Developmental Disabilities Assistance and
Bill of Rights Act of 2000 (PL No. 106-402)*

Federal Law and Disability

Disabilities laws are civil rights laws and evolved from the Civil Rights Act of 1964. Since then, disabilities law has developed to now address the complex and comprehensive issues affecting self-determination, independence, and self-sufficiency of people with disabilities. Federal law also addresses the rapid development of assistive technology (AT) and people with disabilities. Both areas of the law—disabilities and assistive technology—have had a dramatic effect on communication and participation opportunities for people with ASD. From birth to age twenty-one, people with disabilities are entitled to a great many of the tools and services needed to facilitate maximum participation in our society. It is very important to provide AAC to people in need as soon as possible and certainly early in the school years. Let's look at some of the laws that address people with communication disabilities and the assistive technology to which they are entitled.

Sections 504 & 508 of the Rehabilitation Act of 1993

Accommodations to insure equal opportunity can comprise services and devices such as AAC. The Rehabilitation Act of 1973 (PL 93-112), amended in 1993, includes Section 504, which is a federal law that prohibits any agency (including school systems) that receives federal money from discriminating against a person because of her disability. Section 504 requires that the agency provide reasonable accommodations so that services and benefits to people with disabilities are equal to and as effective as services to non-disabled people. Section 508 of this law requires federal agencies to make electronic and information technology accessible to people with disabilities.

Americans with Disabilities Act (ADA)

The Americans with Disabilities Act (ADA) of 1990 (PL No. 101-336) states that individuals with disabilities must be afforded the same opportunities to participate in our society and obtain the same benefit from that participation as their peers without disabilities. For some people with autism, an AAC device may facilitate greater participation and therefore greater access to the benefits available in our society.

Individuals with Disabilities Education Act (IDEA)

The first law specifically addressing the needs of children with disabilities was Public Law 94-142, the Education of All Handicapped Children Act, passed in 1975. Since its inception, this law has been reauthorized and amended several times, and, as of December 2004, it is known as Public Law 108-446, the Individuals with Disabilities Education Improvement Act (IDEIA). Henceforth we will refer to it in this book as IDEA 2004. However, since regulations for IDEA 2004 have not yet been written, most of the information included in this chapter on special education law references IDEA 1997 (PL 105-017).

IDEA dictates that in order for a state to receive federal funds, it must provide each child with disabilities in their state a free and appropriate public education (FAPE). Furthermore, IDEA states that "Each public agency shall ensure that assistive technology devices or assistive technology services, or both, are made available to a child with a disability." In IDEA 2004, the importance of assistive technology was stated as follows: "The education of children with disabilities can be made more effective by... supporting the development and use of technology, including assistive technology devices and assistive technology services, to maximize accessibility for children with disabilities."

Federal Laws and State Regulations

As mentioned, by the time this book goes to press, the regulations for IDEA 2004, also known as IDEIA or PL 108-446, will not have been written by the federal government nor will they be interpreted and implemented by the states. Although states are required to comply with the federal laws, each state may address and interpret these laws somewhat differently; ultimately, state law overrides federal law. It is important for parents and professionals to stay informed concerning the status of the federal regulations and their state's interpretation of them. The following websites offer frequent updates about IDEA 2004's new regulations, including those regarding assistive technology and augmentative & alternative communication: http://www.ideapractices.org; http://www.cec.sped.org/pp/.

Federal Laws Specific to Assistive Technology

The federal laws discussed above, including all versions of IDEA, Sections 504 and 508, ADA, and the Telecommunications Act of 1996 (requires manufacturers of telecommunication equipment to ensure that equipment is accessible to people with disabilities), involve major assistive technology components. The following laws are assistive technology laws in and of themselves.

The Technology Related Assistance for Individuals with Disabilities Act (Tech Act, USC PL 100-407) of 1988 was a groundbreaking piece of legislation that significantly improved the lives of people with disabilities. Assistive technology was finally recognized as a powerful tool for people with disabilities. This law is written broadly enough to include existing assistive technology and potential advances in AT.

The Assistive Technology Act (ATA) of 2004 (PL 108-364) funds fifty-six state programs designed to address the assistive technology (and AAC) needs of people with disabilities. This act ensures that people with disabilities will have access to the assistive technology devices and services they need while their service providers, educators, and employers will be provided the appropriate training. In addition, the new ATA promises there will be permanent, ongoing financial support for assitive technology programs. The following website provides updated information on the implementation of this law: http://www.ataporg.org.

What Do These Laws Mean to You as a Parent or Practitioner?

First, under federal law, AT devices and services must be available for every child who can benefit from them in every state. Second, federal law is clear that people with disabilities are entitled to any services and supports, including AAC, that ensure their equal opportunity to the benefits of society. These benefits include self-determination, independence, and participation as fully as possible. Federal law mandates that people with disabilities participate in normalized and least restrictive environments.

IDEA is specific about who is eligible for AAC. According to this law, every child is entitled to a "free and appropriate public education" (FAPE). "Free," of course, means at no cost to parents. "Appropriate" can be a subjective term and sometimes becomes a bone of contention between parents and educators. Essentially, it means the education provided for a student with a disability should result in measurable progress in areas that improve quality of life. "Appropriate" in this context also

means that the educational methods, tools, and environments may require adaptation so that measurable progress in the skills needed for communication and participation, including academics, can occur. Your child is eligible for AAC if an AAC tool or device facilitates access to a "free and appropriate public education."

What is an AAC *Service* and What Does it Include?

You'll note that the law specifies that assistive technology devices *and* services be considered for every child with a disability, regardless of how mild or severe her disability. IDEA defines AAC as a tool *and* a service. An AAC *service* involves an evaluation of the need for AAC and extends to providing the actual AAC device or tool deemed necessary. The service also includes training the student in the use of AAC and training all staff who have contact with the child. The law also mandates parent training in the use of the AAC tool or device. In addition, technical assistance on using, modifying, or customizing the AAC device or tool all falls under the category of "services." Technical support to family and caregivers is necessary to ensure that the AAC tool or device is used appropriately and effectively.

What Entitlement to an AAC Service Means

- Evaluation of the need for AAC
- Providing the AAC devices or tools
- Training the student
- Training the staff
- Training the parents
- Modifying, repairing, customizing the AAC
- Replacing the AAC tools or device when needed
- Considering the need for AAC at each IEP meeting
- Evaluating the effectiveness of the AAC at each IEP meeting

How is Eligibility for AAC Determined?

Individualized Family Service Plans (IFSP)

Infants and toddlers in birth to three-year-old special education programs have what is called an Individualized Family Service Plan (IFSP). An IFSP is a family-focused, written document that guides the early intervention process for infants and toddlers with disabilities. The IFSP entitles a family to the supports needed to facilitate the development of their child within the child's natural environments; namely, the family itself, childcare setting, and the community.

AAC is indicated for those children who have difficulties with the primary tasks of early childhood, including communication and play. If a child aged zero to three is delayed in communication or play skills and has an IFSP, she is eligible for AAC tools or services as part of her IFSP. Delay is established through parent report, observation by your local early intervention program, and formal testing that generates a report. In this situation, an AAC tool or device can promote more and better communication and interaction between the young child and her family members. An AAC tool may also facilitate the development of interactive play skills—a critical component in the development of learning, communication, and socialization.

Individualized Education Programs (IEP)

The IEP is a written document detailing a highly individualized learning program designed for an individual aged three to twenty-one during their school years. An IEP is drawn up by a team including parents, family members, special and general educators, speech pathologists, and other support services members, such as occupational and physical therapists. The team collaboratively considers the unique learning, communication, and behavioral needs of the student and designs an educational program to address those needs. Each time an IEP team convenes it must consider the need for assistive technology devices or services or evaluate the effectiveness of existing assistive technology. It is important to remember that AAC is not a goal in and of itself, but a means to reach particular goals, such as participation in the school or community.

After age twenty-one, adults with autism can have IHPs or ISPs, Individualized Habilitation Programs or Individualized Service Plans. These function as adult versions of the IEP. AAC is included in these documents as necessary tools for self-determination and participation in work and community life. More information on acquiring AAC for adults is discussed below.

Section 504 Plans

A student with ASD who is functioning at grade level in academics may not have an IEP, yet still need AAC. Section 504 is a civil rights statute that addresses the concept of "equal opportunity" and applies to any institution that receives federal funds, including public schools. Section 504 encompasses a broader definition of disability than IDEA does and therefore may include students with, for example, Asperger's disorder, who may not be eligible for services under IDEA. Section 504 defines a person with disabilities as someone who "has a physical or mental impairment which substantially limits one or more major life activities." These include activities such as hearing, learning, walking, sleeping, speaking, breathing, and working.

Students in 504 programs may require AAC in order to have an equal opportunity to participate in academic and extracurricular programs, benefits, and services. A student with Asperger's, for example, may have difficulty with written communication and benefit greatly from a word processor. The work completed on a word processor may be a more accurate representation of the student's abilities and therefore allow greater levels of participation in academic areas. Section 504 states that services and benefits to students with disabilities must be equal to and as effective as services and benefits afforded other students.

According to federal law, students with 504 plans must be provided with a comprehensive, individualized evaluation of their needs, including regular re-evaluations. Of course, this applies to providing assistive technology and AAC to allow students with disabilities access to FAPE. All of these recommendations must be in writing. The school is also required to provide the appropriate AAC device, as well as the training, repair, and maintenance of the device.

How Can a Child with One of These Plans Access AAC Tools and Services?

In order to have AAC devices and strategies incorporated into your child's IFSP, IEP, or 504 Plan, she must be evaluated. (Extensive information on the assessment process is provided in chapter 4.) Either a parent or the school may request an initial AAC evaluation for a child. Requests must be in writing. If the school system has made the request, the parent must provide written consent for the evaluation to take place. However, regardless of whether an evaluation is requested or not, according to the law, a student's potential need for assistive technology must be considered at *every* IEP and IFSP meeting, whether it is an annual review or a meeting to revise a program. In fact, considering AT and AAC must be an ongoing process. This goes for students who are already using AAC and those who aren't. People grow and change and new technologies and methods develop continually, so no opportunity to consider AAC should be overlooked.

What Does IDEA Say About AAC Evaluations?

IDEA is very clear about when, where, and how AAC evaluations are to be conducted. As mentioned, AAC must be considered each and every time an IEP is written. Diagnostic observations, evaluations, and assessments, in order to be an accurate reflection of a child's strengths and needs, must be conducted in the natural environment—the environment in which the child learns, plays, works, and interacts with others. Children and adults with autism, like the rest of us, are most comfortable in their natural environment, and evaluations conducted here are most representative of their actual communication needs. In this way, then, the natural environment becomes an important part of the assessment, and the AAC intervention will be designed around the needs identified in those environments. Assessments and evaluations can be formal, using the instruments mentioned in chapter 4, or they may be more informal, diagnostic observations. Some school districts do an AAC "preview" first, observing the student to see if AAC is appropriate before they conduct a more lengthy evaluation.

Federal Timelines and Assessments

A communication system is a basic human right and if a parent or practitioner believes someone with autism can benefit from AAC, time without a communication system must be minimized. Indeed, without a means to communicate, many people with ASD develop inappropriate ways to communicate in a desperate effort to express their needs. Identifying the need for AAC, evaluating the AAC user, and selecting or developing an AAC system should occur in a timely manner.

Keep in mind, when it comes to implementing AAC, federal timelines are subject to state interpretation. That said, let's look at what federal law dictates concerning timelines. Federal law applies to both IEPs (ages three to twenty-one) and IFSPs (birth to three). If a parent or practitioner believes their student can benefit from AAC, they should put in a written request for an AAC evaluation right away. If the request comes from the practitioners, the parent must first give consent for the evaluation. In any case, from the time the parent has signed the consent or made the request herself, there is a sixty-day (including weekends and holidays) timeline for the evaluation to be completed. (This is a shorter timeline from old IDEA, which was ninety days). There is another thirty-day timeline from then to the approval of the IEP with AAC included. After the approval of the IEP, AAC must be provided as soon as possible. Please note, however, individual states have the option to adjust these timelines according to their specific regulations. Since state regulations are binding, parents and practitioners are wise to be aware of their home state's interpretation of IDEA 2004 (IDEIA). The following website gives up-to-date information on the status of timelines in the new IDEA 2004: www.cec.sped.org.

Getting the Right Assessment

Integral to the process of considering AAC is an IEP team member with expertise in the field of AAC. Many public and private school systems have assistive technology and AAC teams that provide the evaluations, expertise, and training to practitioners. There are several organizations that provide "certification" in AAC and universities that offer graduate courses and degrees in AT, including AAC. However, there are many practitioners—namely, special educators, SLPs, OTs, and PTs—who have expertise in AAC without formal certification or a degree, and experience in the field of AAC is valid as well. This person must have knowledge and experience in the range of AAC options, from the most simple picture board to the most complex voice output device. If no person on the IEP team has expertise in AAC, then the team must reconvene after gathering the necessary information concerning the most current systems and tools available and how they will apply to their particular student. Like IEP teams, 504 teams must include people with expertise in both the disability and the AT options available.

You may contact your state's Department of Education for information on contacting local qualified AT specialists. The American Speech and Language Association can also refer you to therapists with expertise in AAC. Finally, the QIAT Consortium (Quality Indicators for Assistive Technology Services), an Internet website and discussion board, can provide information on assessment practices and practitioners in your area (http://www.qiat.org).

It is safe to say that with the passage of the various federal laws regarding technology, every state has an AT department and practitioners, so it is unlikely there will be no qualified individuals available. What is more likely is that the AT teams may be short-staffed and have a backlog of referrals to deal with. In these cases, schools must abide by federally mandated timelines.

Even if the school has a tech team but as a parent you don't agree with the results of your child's AAC assessment done by the school, you can seek out a private AAC practitioner to conduct an assessment. In this case, the school should pay for the outside service. If your child's team agrees with the new assessment recommendations, the school will "accept" the new findings and is required to put *those* AAC recommendations into place. If, as a parent, you feel your child has not received the AT needed for him to be successful in school under Section 504, you may file for a due process hearing. In situations where a child has not received technology necessary to access his education, parents may file a complaint with the Office of Civil Rights.

Ultimately, decisions concerning all educational programming, including AAC interventions, are made by the IEP team and not any one individual. But as a parent, you have the right to appeal those decisions. In this case, mediation is the next step in resolving the conflict. By law, you should be provided information about how to proceed with conflict resolution at the start of each IEP meeting.

Things can run amok when a school system has no tech team or awareness of the power of AAC and the legal requirement to provide it. Unfortunately, problems can arise when a school is uninformed, ill-equipped, or otherwise unprepared to deal with an AAC intervention. Often in this case, motivated parents will do their own research on AAC tools and determine that the school should purchase a sophisticated, expensive voice output device, thinking that a higher tech device will promote more and better communication for their child. As mentioned in chapter 3, this is not typically the case. Most often, a low-tech device is the best first tool.

The IEP Team's Role in an AAC Intervention

Aside from including an AAC expert on your team, IDEA requires that if the student is included in a general education setting, her general education teachers be involved in the process of considering AAC as well as in the resulting training. This ensures that the AAC device will be integrated into the child's general education program if the child is so included.

Each IEP team member, including parents, family members, special and regular educators, occupational, physical, speech and language therapists, *and* the potential AAC user has the right, if she is able, to participate in team decision-making. The team approach dictates that meetings be scheduled to accommodate the key players in the child's school life.

Changes to IDEA 1997

IDEA 2004 has made several changes to streamline the IEP process. These changes are described in the summaries below. It is important to keep informed as to your individual state's regulations concerning these changes and consult the referenced websites for frequent updates.

- An IEP team member may be excused from attending the IEP meeting if the subject matter does not address that member's area of concern and both the parents and school have agreed. Parent's agreement must be in writing.
- After the annual IEP meeting, changes to the IEP may be made through a written document, and without holding a meeting, if parents and school agree.
- Actual physical meetings are no longer required. IEP meetings may be held through video conferencing and conference phone calls.

Considering the Need for AAC

At each meeting, team members should ask the following questions as part of considering the need for AAC. These questions are basic for any student, whether they are an AAC user or not.

Questions to Consider for a Student without AAC Supports

1. What developmentally appropriate tasks is the child unable to do that AAC may enable her to do? For a preschool child, this might be selecting a play center. For a primary school aged child, interacting with peers or responding to a question in class. And for a high school student, participating in a cooperative learning group with her peers or completing a writing assignment.
2. What particular AAC tool would enable the child to engage in these tasks? (See chapter 3 and the resource guide for types of devices available.)
3. Is AAC needed to effectively address any IEP goals or objectives? For example, greeting teachers or peers, following a schedule, staying on task, answering questions, requesting a break, or accessing the general education curriculum.

4. Would AAC facilitate the child's participation in a less restrictive environment, such as in a general education class, outside on the playground, or attending her neighborhood school?
5. Would an AAC tool or device help the child communicate more effectively; i.e., requesting help from a teacher or playing an interactive board game with a peer?
6. Would an AAC device ensure that the child would need less support from practitioners, staff, or family members? For example, would it allow her to follow a visual schedule independently or request particular items in the school lunchroom without assistance?
7. Would AAC give the person skills that are important to her peers and family? This might mean asking for a turn at bat on the playground or managing leisure time productively and independently at home.

Questions to Consider for a Student with an Existing AAC System

1. Considering the AAC based communication objectives on the IEP and the corresponding data, is there measurable and meaningful progress? If so, identify the supports to achieve the next level of communicative competence; i.e., increasing vocabulary, involving more communication partners, transitioning to a VOCA or a more complex device.
2. If there is no significant measurable progress, ask: Where are the breakdowns in successfully meeting these objectives? This might be inadequate data collection, use of an inappropriate AAC tool, device, or symbol system, a lack of opportunity to use AAC, minimal opportunities to communicate planned by communication partners, a need for more staff training, improper device maintenance, etc.

3. Are there new developmentally appropriate skills that this student needs to achieve? How can AAC support the development of those skills?
4. Are there new IEP objectives that AAC can support?
5. Are there new skills that would enable her to participate in a less restrictive environment or with less support from practitioners? How can AAC support the development of these skills?
6. Are there new skills that are important to family and peers that AAC may facilitate?

How is AAC Integrated Into a Child's Educational Plan?

AAC can be included as a particular part of the child's IEP or IFSP and 504 plan. It can be a general education modification or a related service, such as is provided by speech or occupational therapists. AAC can also be included as a means to address a goal or objective, for example, "Kwon will answer "wh" questions in social studies using his AAC device."

Some school districts do not permit using the name of a commercial AAC product on an IEP. This is not a problem as long as the IEP objectives include mentioning an AAC device and the context

within which it is to be used. For example, "Calvin will use his VOCA to select a leisure activity." It is important that IEP objectives are stated in this way so that practitioners are clear about how and where the device will be used. In addition, measuring communication outcomes is easier and more evident with clear objectives.

For older children and youth, AAC can be included in an IEP as part of transition services to prepare the student for independent life. For example, "Latoya will use her AAC device to access a neighborhood restaurant." A student's transition team, the collaboration of the school system and vocational agencies, is responsible for seeing that AAC devices and services are in place and integral to the transition process.

Transition Planning and AAC

Consideration of the need for and the evaluation of existing AAC is especially important for transition points in a student's life. IDEA requires that transition goals be included in the IEP beginning at age sixteen and addressed at each subsequent IEP meeting. If a student has an AAC device for school, planning must occur during the later school years to include the AAC device and supports as part of the transition into the adult environment. Your state's vocational rehabilitation agency should be involved in all transition planning with the school.

The Assistive Technology Act of 2004 addresses the needs of adult AAC users entering the workforce. The AT Act funds programs that implement technical assistance and training for students who are transitioning from school to work. (More information on how to obtain funding for AAC devices for adults with ASD is discussed below.) If a student has acquired a device from her school, the vocational rehabilitation agency can purchase the existing device from the school at graduation or purchase one outright on its own. During this transition period, the need for AAC continues as part of the IEP as well as on the IHP (Individualized Habilitation Program) or ISP (Individualized Service Plan) developed by the vocational or rehabilitation agency receiving the student. The US Department of Education encourages cooperation between the school and vocational agency, and, in particular, the transfer of AT devices from school to workplace.

Funding for AAC Devices and Services

There are well over twenty federal and state programs and agencies that provide funding for AAC. There are private health insurance and nonprofit foundations that can provide funding for AAC as well. Usually, the local educational agency (LEA) pays for the AAC devices for students ages three to twenty-one. In this case, AAC is indicated on the IEP as necessary for achieving measurable progress on goals and objectives or participating in a less restrictive environment. If a student is eligible for Medicaid, the school system can apply for AAC through Medicaid. Remember, AAC tools and devices can be as inexpensive as a notepad or more costly than a personal computer. Voice output AAC can range in price from ten dollars to over ten thousand dollars. Regardless of who pays for the device, for school-aged children, according to the law, the school is responsible for the evaluation, and machine maintenance and repair. In addition, IDEA dictates that the school provide the student, staff, and parents training in the use of the device. A school is not permitted to deny providing an AAC device based on its cost alone. However, if there are two appropriate AAC tool or device options and one is more costly than the other, the school has the right to purchase the less expensive device as long as it provides "measurable and meaningful" benefit to the child.

What Does "Measurable and Meaningful Benefit" Mean?

Measurable benefit, a benchmark of all special education best practice (including AAC) and mandated by law, means that an educational or communication program must be designed in a way that allows the student to acquire communication skills that are greater than those she had prior to the AAC, and that increase can be measured. Measurable benefit requires the following:

1. Communication objectives are defined as observable and measurable. (E.g., "Andy will use his VOCA to ask for help.")
2. Present levels of performance on the identified objectives are measured. (Presently Andy screams when he needs help. Incidence of screaming for help is eight times per day.)
3. AAC interventions are designed that address the acquisition of the communication objectives on the IEP. (A single switch VOCA with the message "I need help" is placed on Andy's desk. Staff model its use by activating it prior to Andy's screaming.)
4. Data is collected regularly to determine if measurable progress is resulting from the AAC intervention. (Data is collected on the incidence of screaming per day, without AAC at baseline, and with AAC.)
5. AAC intervention is adjusted to ensure measurable benefit. (E.g., if Andy's incidence of screaming has not decreased, staff is instructed to give more modeled prompts to use AAC.)

Measurable benefit is a very important concept and applies not only to IEPs and students with autism but in accessing AAC for adults with autism. There is a strong case for outcomes-based decision making in terms of funding AAC devices. Practitioners and parents will have to show hard data indicating that AAC provides a measurable benefit and that these benefits are cost effective and in essence the AAC "pays for itself." For example, if AAC enables an adult with autism to communicate functionally, her prospects for working and participating in the community are greatly improved.

You will note that I have also included the word "meaningful" in "measurable, meaningful benefit." The word "meaningful" is used to emphasize the importance of using AAC to increase communication and participation, and not for labeling or drilling. Identifying PCS on a communication board is not communication and is not *meaningful*.

Funding Options for AAC Through Early Intervention

For children ages zero to three, the early intervention program through your local school district is responsible for purchasing your child's AAC device or tool. The early intervention program will seek funding secured through third party sources (private insurance) and Medicaid. If the early intervention program is not successful in acquiring funding for the AAC device, then responsibility for the purchase falls to them. It is important to note, however, that the family and the early intervention program must pursue every funding option, including purchasing used or recycled AAC equipment, before the early intervention program is obliged to pay for equipment. Even the manufacturer of the device will assist in seeking funding options. If third party funding pays for 51 percent of the device or more, the AAC device belongs to the family and cannot be used by any other child. If the early intervention program funds 51 percent of the device, the early intervention program owns it and it can be used by other children.

In most early intervention programs there are AAC tools and devices that are part of the environment and are used in structured small group and individual communication instruction. For example, Mrs. Myers is doing a cookie making activity with her toddler group. She has a VOCA with the following two messages: "Put on sprinkles" and "I want to eat a cookie." Mrs. Myers structures the activity so that each student uses the VOCA to participate in the activity. The VOCA is shared by all the students and each has the opportunity to use language *and* benefit from the modeling of language provided by the VOCA through Mrs. Myers and his peers. In this case, the AAC device is part of the classroom and not devoted to just one child. At this young age, in an environment richly engineered for communication, sharing a low- or high-tech AAC device does not appear to impede language acquisition.

Obtaining Devices for School-aged Children Through Medicaid

Each state has a Medicaid agency and specific procedures for AAC funding for eligible school-aged children. Remember to check your individual state's regulations concerning Medicaid. A family must qualify for Medicaid based on economic need. In general, Medicaid provides some or all funding for AAC (categorized as durable medical equipment and referred to as speech generating devices) if AAC is considered medically necessary rather than educationally necessary.

It is important to note that in some states, Medicaid will fund an AAC device but will require a three- to four-year span of time before they fund another device for the same person. Therefore, school systems will not apply for Medicaid until they are certain that they have identified the most appropriate device for the individual. This often occurs during the high school years, when the AAC user has had the opportunity to "grow" with increasingly more complex devices until finally the most appropriate device is identified for her.

The procedure for obtaining AAC through Medicaid involves many players and extensive paperwork. The process can be started within the school system or by parent request. A speech pathologist or assistive technology specialist must conduct an evaluation to determine if AAC is indeed medically necessary. Medical necessity must be carefully documented. In addition, a referral or prescription for AAC from the child's primary care physician or pediatrician is necessary. A recent copy of a speech and language assessment, a psychological assessment, and an educational assessment is also needed. Last and most important is a letter from a speech and language pathologist or AAC specialist justifying the need for the AAC device. The report provided for Medicaid must also include information on trials with specific devices, a treatment plan, and goals and objectives. It is recommended that if you are denied, rework your justification section and re-apply for funding.

It is important to note that AAC devices procured through Medicaid are the property of the student and will transition to each of the student's new environments. These AAC devices cannot be used by any other student.

Other Funding Options to Consider

If it is not possible to secure funding through the school system, state Medicaid services, or third party payment, your child's pediatrician can write a prescription for an AAC device. In this case the physician must indicate that AAC is medically necessary. For example, Tara, a three-year-old, non-speaking child has a potentially fatal food allergy. She will need the device to let others know what she can and cannot eat. In this case, funding can be obtained through the Early and Periodic Screening, Diagnosis, and Treatment Program (EPSDT), which is part of the federal Medicaid program. In order to apply for funding through EPSDT, the following is needed: a physician's prescription, a letter of medical necessity from a qualified medical professional (such as a speech pathologist), the child's medical history, diagnosis, and prognosis, and medical justification for the AAC device. The school system will initiate and follow through on all procedures needed to obtain an AAC device through Medicaid and EPSDT.

Obtaining AAC for Adults with Autism

Obtaining AAC for adults with autism is more difficult than accessing AAC for students ages zero to twenty-one since AAC devices and services for adults are not considered "entitlements." The process for adults often involves tapping more than one funding source, namely Medicaid, Social Security, health insurance, loans, and federal entitlement programs for people with disabilities. At age eighteen, every person with a communication disability is eligible for Medicaid and potentially an AAC device. Medicaid is defined differently by each state and the extent to which AAC devices and services are provided and reimbursed is state specific. In general, Medicaid can provide an AAC device if it is deemed medically necessary. AAC is then labeled a "speech generating device" and is considered "durable medical equipment." The Medicaid procedures described above for school-aged children will also apply to adults with developmental disabilities who require AAC.

Adults with autism can have IHPs or ISPs, Individualized Habilitation Programs or Individualized Service Plans, adult versions of the IEP. AAC is included in these documents as necessary tools for self-determination and participation in work and community life. Besides Medicaid, funding sources can be accessed under the Rehabilitation Act Amendments of 1992 if AAC is shown to support employment and independent living. AAC can also be accessed through both Sections 504 and 508. People may also purchase their own AAC device with the help of the Assistive Technology Act (ATA) of 2004. This Act provides alternative funding to allow people with disabilities to purchase AAC through low-interest loans or interest buy-down programs, revolving loan funds, and loan guarantees or insurance programs. Other means of financial assistance to purchase AAC include Social Security Work Incentive programs, Medicare for the Working Disabled, and Internal Revenue deductions.

Commonly Asked Questions

Regardless of the best intentions of school districts, professionals, and parents, AAC evaluations and interventions can have their share of problems. Sometimes they raise more questions than answers. Let's review some commonly asked questions and look at some potential pitfalls to see how they can be effectively handled.

What if a parent doesn't agree with the outcome of their child's AAC evaluation?

If an AAC evaluation is conducted and a parent does not agree with the recommendations, she can appeal the decision. If she can prove that the results are skewed, an independent evaluation should be conducted at the expense of the school system. The IEP team must consider the results of the independent evaluation. If everyone on the IEP team disagrees with the independent evaluation except the parent, the parent can request mediation or file for due process. Mediation is a process whereby a trained person, who is impartial to both parents and the school system, helps both parties come to an agreement about the IEP and the AAC system. A parent may also request a due process hearing with a judge to resolve a dispute between them and the school system. School systems are required by law to provide parents with the information needed to file for due process. Although this process can be unpleasant, there are instances where a parent's knowledge of their child's potential as a communicator is more comprehensive and accurate than that of the school team.

Can my child use her AAC device outside of school?

Children in early intervention and three to twenty-one special education programs are expected to use their AAC in all settings, regardless of who technically owns the device. Use outside of the school setting is beneficial and will promote more rapid development of communication and generalization of communication skills. It takes time and many positive experiences with AAC for the user with autism to view AAC as powerful and indeed her "voice."

What if the school purchased the AAC device?

If a child uses an AAC device that has been purchased by her school because it provides access to a "free and appropriate public education," the law requires that the device also be used at home. The AAC device will enable the student to communicate with her family about the school day, complete homework, and share any prob-

lems that may be occurring. It is important that this arrangement be clearly stated in the child's IEP so that both parents and practitioners send the device back and forth between home and school.

Who is responsible for the care and maintenance of the AAC device when the school has purchased it?

If using an AAC device is built into a child's IEP, the school is responsible for routine maintenance and care, updating, and replacing the device if need be, even if the device is regularly taken home. If a device is being repaired, it is the responsibility of the school to provide your child an alternative AAC device in the interim. If an AAC device appears to be abused, the school or zero to three program must determine whether the problem is due to lack of understanding or actual abuse. The IEP team then reconvenes to troubleshoot the problem. The team may determine that the parents require additional training or that there are other ways to meet the IEP objective, perhaps with a low-tech device or communication board.

It is important that parents, school staff, and students take joint responsibility for care and maintenance of the AAC device. Practitioners report that the more parents are invested in the care and use of the device, the better communication partners they are to their child. Of course, the collaboration between home and school results in the most benefit to the student.

If a family purchases an AAC device for their child can they send it to school?

A child's school system cannot require her family to purchase a device, nor can they require a child to bring a family-purchased AAC device to school, but, parents can freely send their child's AAC device to school. If the IEP team deems the family-bought device inappropriate for the student, the school is not obligated to provide training or use the device. Parents can, of course, appeal this decision. If the parents are seeing their child use the device communicatively at home, they may ask for an IEP meeting to show data or a videotape of their child using the device. Incidentally, the US Department of Education states that if parents send an AAC device to school that they themselves purchased and it is broken while the child is on the bus or during school hours, the school system is responsible for those repairs.

Why would a family purchase a device when it is the financial responsibility of the school?

There are some advantages to buying a device yourself. First, you may not have to shell out your own money, considering there are many available funding resources that can be tapped. When a family makes the time and energy investment, AAC is more likely to be used at home. Furthermore, when the family purchases the device, it will obviously have more control over its use.

I've tried every avenue of funding for my child's AAC device and run into dead ends. Who can help me?

If a parent or practitioner is having difficulty accessing funding for AAC, either through their school system or Medicaid, it is reasonable to seek legal help. Many states have private nonprofit law firms that are designated as protection and advocacy systems for people with disabilities. The National Association of Protection and Advocacy Systems, Inc., referenced in the resource list in the appendix, can direct parents and practitioners to Legal and Advocacy Disabilities Services in each state.

The school is conscientiously using the AAC device but there is no follow through at home. What can be done?

There are instances when families are not invested in using the AAC device. Often times, these families have developed their own distinctive communication system, (such as a combination of manual signs, gestures, and vocalizations) with their child before any device was put into place. It is important for practitioners to honor the family's unique system. Although it may not be understood outside the family, it is likely very effective within it. One of the goals of AAC is to enhance existing functional communication. Practitioners can provide family support by offering after-school AAC in-services to supplement and enhance the system the family already has in place.

What can a parent ask for to ensure the best AAC results for their child?

Parents should ask their school to:

1. Fully integrate the device into their child's school day.
2. Provide an extended year program so that communication skills are constantly being reinforced.
3. Train parents in the use and programming of the device.
4. Train staff in device operation, programming, and curricular adaptations.
5. Commit to assigning daily homework to improve AAC skills and foster communication between their child, themselves, and the school.

(Adapted from Golinker, 2005)

What happens to the AAC device when a child transitions to a new school?

If a child continues to need her school-bought device for communication, participation, or to address IEP goals and objectives, the device should go with the child to the new educational setting until the new school can purchase another one. At this point, the old device goes back to the original school who owns it. Because the "sending" school is often reluctant to allow the student to keep her device until the "receiving" school purchases one like it, IEP transition plans should address this issue with plenty of time to spare. In cases when a child is using less costly communication tools, such as communication boards, communication wallets, picture exchange books, activity schedule books, and similar visual communication and cueing tools, the current teacher can send the actual tools or copy them for the student to use at her new school or district. It is important for both the sending and receiving school to cooperate in providing as seamless a transition as possible, where there will be no interruption of the child's communication system. The temporary absence of a communication system for a person with severe communication impairments is like taking away her ears and voice!

What responsibility do private schools have to provide AAC for children with ASD?

AAC must be provided for a child in a non-public school only if the child was placed there as a result of an IEP decision. This decision might be made if the child's local public school system does not have the appropriate program or supports for her. It is the public school system's responsibility to seek out and evaluate children in these placements and provide the same level of consideration, evaluation, assessment, purchase, training, maintenance, and support, as mandated by law and provided for children in public schools.

What other rights do parents and caregivers of AAC users have?

- Parents have the right to discuss with their child's teacher, school staff and administrators, and IEP and IFSP team members why they think AAC will benefit their child.
- Parents have the right to an independent AAC evaluation if they do not agree with the one provided by the school. The school must consider the findings of the independent AAC evaluator.
- Parents have the right to be involved in decision-making in terms of the need for AAC, the type of tool or device, the time and place of AAC parent training, and any maintenance, updates, or adjustments made to the device, including selecting vocabulary.
- Parents have the right to information about the range of AAC possibilities, from no-tech communication boards to high-tech voice output devices.
- Parents have the right to advocacy. This means that the parents can bring an advocate or support person to their IEP meetings to ensure that their child receives what she needs. There are special education organizations that provide advocates at no charge. There are also pro-bono attorneys who provide free advocacy services.

- Parents have the right to purchase an AAC device and if the IEP team agrees that the device is appropriate, the parents have a right to receive the range of AAC services including training, maintenance, upgrading, and repair. If the IEP team does not agree that the device is appropriate, parents may use the device at home but cannot expect the device to be used in the school setting.
- Parents have the right to training in the use of the AAC device. This training is part of the "assistive technology service" mentioned in federal regulations and is provided for by the school system.
- Parents have the right to privacy and confidentiality according to the Family Educational Rights and Privacy Act. This means that none of the IEP team members can divulge any information or decisions made regarding the student and the AAC tool or device recommended without permission of the parents.

Conclusion

The US government has a thirty-plus-year history of providing legal supports to make it possible for people with disabilities to participate more fully in society. Communication is the core deficit in autism and what human beings need most for self-realization is the ability and opportunity to communicate. Considering that AAC helps people develop functional communication, it is likely that the majority of people on the autism spectrum can benefit from AAC. And it is tragic to consider the number of people with autism, now adults, who have not had the opportunity for self-realization through communication because they had no access to AAC.

Currently there is strong federal support for assistive technology and AAC. Federal law mandates that every citizen have the right to self-determination, independence, self-sufficiency, and access to the benefits of our society. AAC can provide the supports needed to realize these benefits. Parents and practitioners need to work as partners and stay abreast of federal law and state regulations. In addition, it is critical that Congress keep its promise and fully fund IDEA 2004 (IDIEA) and continue to provide AAC communication and participation supports for people with ASD.

6 | Conclusion & Future Projections

This book is designed as an overview of AAC and autism—a primer—a resource for basic information about AAC and to jump-start one's thinking about interventions. It is not meant to be a "cookbook" or manual of how-tos. The appendix of this book provides information on helpful resources such as training opportunities, conferences, web sites, journals, and AAC associations that can further your knowledge.

There are many key concepts that parents and practitioners should understand in creating and designing AAC interventions for people with ASD. Several points discussed in this primer are worth reviewing:

1. *The right to communicate extends to all people.* Providing AAC for a limited or non-speaker with ASD is not a luxury, it is essential and must be provided immediately.

2. *There are no cognitive or language prerequisites for beginning most AAC interventions.* Often people who are the most disabled by ASD have the most hidden potential as communicators.

3. *AAC does four important things:*
   - It enhances existing functional communication.
   - It provides an alternative to nonexistent speech communication.

- It provides supports for the development of language for people with autism who have no symbolic language.
- It stimulates more complex language, and communication development and use for limited communicators.

4. *Verbal language is not inhibited by AAC.* Current research, although limited, suggests that AAC actually increases interaction, increases motivation for communication, and increases vocalization and speech (Cafiero, 2004; Dexter, 1998).

5. *Communication involves two people:* the communication partners. The speaking partner must provide **input,** or receptive language stimulation by pairing speech with visual symbols (or written words). This encourages the non-speaking communication partner to learn to generate **output.** Input is equally important with regard to no-tech, low tech, or high-tech AAC tools.

6. *AAC is about communication.* It should not be used for quizzing or rote learning of symbols. The only time it is acceptable to use AAC in a non-interactive way is if the user has adopted the AAC tool as his "real" voice and in addition to using it functionally, needs to use it to do homework or take a test.

7. *More expensive or technically more sophisticated devices are not necessarily better.* For example, voice output devices (VOCAs) are not for everyone. If a person with ASD is more communicative and engaged with voice output and is not distracted by it, then a VOCA may stimulate more interaction. In many cases, however, low-tech devices and techniques work best.

8. *When designing communication boards, select vocabulary that provides the means for interaction.* Be sure not to limit vocabulary only to "words they know." Include new words and new concepts and use the communication intervention as the means to teach those words and concepts.

9. *AAC assessments and interventions are always works in progress.* Assessments, whether formal or informal, must be administered any time there is a change in communication partners, a change in environments, progress in literacy development or general maturity. It is a fluid process, above all.

10. *Matching an AAC tool or device to a person with ASD is an individualized process.* Regardless of how similar two people with autism may be, their communication needs related to their strengths and deficits, communication partners, and environments will be different.

11. *AAC interventions, by law, include devices and services.* Services include training in the use and programming of AAC for parents and practitioners, and maintenance of the AAC device.

12. *There is a progression of AAC tools from the most simple for the developmentally young to increasingly more complex for developmentally older students.* However, students with ASD who are having behavioral or cognitive difficulties may benefit from a more simple, direct way to communicate and need a single symbol for picture exchange whereas they were previously using a communication board with multiple symbols. Communication partners need to be flexible and provide the appropriate AAC tool, even if it seems less complex than what has been used previously.

13. *AAC, if is it truly the voice and ears of a person with ASD, must be portable and accessible.* AAC tools and devices are everyday, practical tools. Regardless of how expensive an AAC tool is or how fragile you may think it is, there is no good reason not to use it in a particular environment. AAC should be used in all communication environments, from classrooms to theme parks.

14. *Don't give up regardless of how slow the progress may be!* Continue to provide receptive language stimulation by pairing speech with visual symbols.

Future Projections in AAC for People with Autism

Often thought to be non-communicative and antisocial, people with autism are now being given an opportunity to learn to express who they are through AAC. The most significant advance in AAC and autism is the often surprising emergence of communication from people who were believed to be cognitively and linguistically incapable of expressive language. AAC is breaking down some of the stereotypes that researchers and practitioners long held about people most severely disabled by their autism.

AAC is a field that is literally exploding with new technologies. Advances in information technology, including the Internet, have provided an effective communication vehicle for people on the autism spectrum. E-mail is a simple cued, concrete, and stationary communication medium and many people with ASD are articulate communicators using this medium. For Internet users without developed literacy skills, PCS can be transmitted through the Internet with the program Inter_Comm® (Mayer-Johnson). More complex, sophisticated communication systems such as Min-Speak are currently being explored as a communication medium for people with autism.

Disabilities law, IDEA 2004, and ADA are requiring that people with autism receive the tools and services they need to participate as fully as possible in their homes, schools, workplaces, and communities. AAC is an essential component of this process. Our vision and our dream is that advances in AAC will unlock and develop the communicative potential of all people affected by autism.

References

Abrams, K. & Cafiero, J. (1991). *Aided Language Stimulation Really Works!* Paper presented at the Mid-Atlantic Augmentative Communication Association Conference. Abstract retrieved from authors.

Acredolo, L. & Goodwyn, S. (2000). *Baby Minds: Brain Building Games Your Baby Will Love.* New York: Bantam Books.

Baker, B. (1986). Using images to generate speech. *Byte, 3,* 160-168.

Beukelman, D. & Mirenda, P. (1998). *Augmentative and Alternative Communication: Management of Severe Communication Disorders in Children and Adults* (2nd ed). Baltimore, MD: Paul H. Brooks.

Blackstone, S. & Berg, M.H. (2003). *Social Networks: A Communication Inventory for Individuals with Complex Communication Needs and their Communication Partners.* Monterey, CA: Augmentative Communication, Inc.

Bondy, A. & Frost, L. (1998). The Picture Exchange Communication System. *Topics in Language Disorders, 19,* 373-390.

Bondy, A. & Frost, L. (2002). *A Picture's Worth: PECS and Other Visual Communication Strategies in Autism.* Bethesda, MD: Woodbine House.

Bransford, J., Brown, A., & Cocking, R. (Eds.) (1999). *How People Learn: Brain, Mind, Experience, and School.* Washington, DC: National Academy Press.

Broderick, A. & Kasa-Hendrickson, C. (2001) Say just one word at first: The emergence of reliable speech in a student labeled with autism. *Journal of the Association for Persons with Severe Handicaps, 26,* 13-24.

Burke, J. & Cerniglia, L. (1990). Stimulus complexity and autistic children's responsivity: Assessing and training a pivotal behavior. *Journal of Autism and Developmental Disorders, 20*(2), 233-253.

Cafiero, J.M. (2001). The effect of an augmentative communication intervention on the communication, language, and academic program of an adolescent with autism. *Focus on Autism and Other Developmental Disabilities, 16(3),* 179-189.

Cafiero, J.M. (1998). Communication power for individuals with autism. *Focus on Autism and Developmental Disabilities, 13,* 113-121.

Cafiero, J.M. (December, 2004). Autism and Literacy: Targeting pre-linguistic behaviors through adapted literature. Unpublished manuscript presented at Autism and Literacy Workshop, Aesthesia Production. New York, New York.

Cafiero, J.M. (1995). The effect of Picture Communication Symbols as a natural language to decrease levels of family stress. Dissertation Abstracts International, UMI. Ann Arbor, MI.

Charlop, M.H., Schreibman, L. & Thibodeau, M.G. (1985). Increasing spontaneous verbal responding in autistic children using a time delay procedure. *Journal of Applied Behavior Analysis 18*: 111-126.

Charlop, M.H. & Trasowech, J.E. (1991). Increasing autistic children's daily spontaneous speech. *Journal of Applied Behavior Analysis 24:* 747-761.

Charlop-Christy, M., Carpenter, M., Le, L., LeBlanc, L. & Kellet, K. (2002). Using the Picture Exchange Communication System (PECS) with children with autism: Assessment of PECS acquisition, speech, social-communicative behavior, and problem behavior. *Journal of Applied Behavior Analysis, 35,* 213-231.

Cumley, G.D. (1997). Introduction of an augmentative and alternative modality: Effects on the quality and quantity of communication interactions of children with severe phonological disorders. Unpublished doctoral dissertation. University of Nebraska, Lincoln.

Dexter, M. (1998). *The effects of aided language stimulation upon verbal output and augmentative communication during storybook reading for children with pervasive developmental disabilities.* Dissertation Abstracts International, UMI. Ann Arbor, MI. 59(5), 1524A.

Falvey, M., Forest, M., Pearpoint, J. & Rosenberg, R. (1994). All My Life's a Circle. In *Using the Tools: Circles, MAP's and PATH.* Toronto, Canada: Inclusion Press.

Forsey, J., Bird, E.K.R., & Bedrosian, J. (1996). Brief Report: The effects of typed and spoken modality combinations on the language performance of adults with autism. *Journal of Autism and Developmental Disorders, 26,* 643-649.

Frost, L., Daly, M., & Bondy, A. (April, 1997). Speech features with and without access to PECS for children with autism. Paper presented at COSAC. Long Beach, NJ.

Frost, L. & Bondy, A. (2001). *The Picture Exchange Communication System (PECS):* 2nd Edition. Newark, DE: Pyramid Educational Products, Inc.

Ganz, J. & Simpson, R. (2004). Effects on communicative requesting and speech development of the Picture Exchange Communication Systems in children with characteristics of autism. *Journal of Autism and Developmental Disorders, 34*(4), 395-409.

Garfin, D. & Lord, C. (1986). Communication as a social problem in autism. In E. Schopler & G. Mesibov (eds.), *Social Behavior in Autism* (pp. 237-261). New York, NY: Plenum Press.

Garrison-Harrel, L., Kamps, D. & Kravits, T. (1997). The effects of peer networks on social-communicative behaviors for students with autism. *Focus on Autism and Other Developmental Disabilities, 12,* 241-254.

Golinker, L. (2005). Getting what you deserve. How to advocate for speech-generating devices and services from the public schools. *Speak Up, 20,* 1, p 11.

Goossens', C., Crain, S.S. & Elder, P. (1999). *Engineering the Pre-School Environment for Interactive Symbolic Communication.* Birmingham, AL: Southeast Augmentative Communication Conference Publications.

Hager, R.M. & Smith, D. (2003). *The public school's special education system as an assistive technology funding source: the cutting edge.* Buffalo, New York: Neighborhood Legal Services. Available online http://www.napas.org and http://www.nls.org.

Johnson, M. (1998). "The Neural Basis of Cognitive Development." In W. Damon, editor-in-chief, D. Kuhn & R. Siegler, volume eds. *Handbook of Child Psychology: Volume 2-Cognition, Perception and Language*, 1-50. New York: John Wiley and Sons.

Koegel, L. (1995). Communication and language intervention. In *Teaching Children with Autism*, R. Koegel & L. Koegel (eds.). Baltimore, MD: Paul H. Brookes Publishers, pp. 17-32.

Light, J. & Binger, C. (1998). *Building Communicative Competence with Individuals Who Use Augmentative and Alternative Communication*. Baltimore, MD: Paul H. Brookes Publishing.

Mayer-Johnson (1994-2005). *The Picture Communication Symbols Libraries, Boardmaker, Writing with Symbols, Inter_Comm*. Mayer-Johnson: Solana Beach, CA: Mayer-Johnson, LLC.

McClannahan, L. & Krantz, P. (1999). *Activity Schedules for Children with Autism: Teaching Independent Behavior*. Bethesda, MD: Woodbine House.

McEachin, J.J., Smith, T. & Lovaas, O.I. (1993). Long-term outcome for children with autism who received early intensive behavioral treatment. *American Journal on Mental Retardation, 97*, 359-372.

Millar, D., Light, J. & Schlosser, R. (2000). The impact of AAC on natural speech development: A meta-analysis. Proceedings of the 9th biennial conference of the International Society for Augmentative and Alternative Communication. Washington, DC: ISAAC, pp. 740-741.

Mirenda, P. & Santogrossi, J. (1985). A prompt-free strategy to teach pictorial communication system use. *Augmentative and Alternative Communication, 1*(4), 143-150.

Mirenda, P., Wilk, D. & Carson, P. (2000). A retrospective analysis of technology use patterns in students with autism over a five-year period. *Journal of Special Education Technology, 15*(3), 5-16.

Mirenda, P. (2003). Toward functional augmentative and alternative communication for students with autism: Manual signs, graphic symbols, and voice output communication aids. *Language, Speech, and Hearing Services in the Schools, 34*, 203-216.

Mirenda, P. (1997). Supporting individuals with challenging behavior through functional communication training and augmentative and alternative communication: A research review. *Augmentative and Alternative Communication, 13,* 207-225.

Mizuko, M., Reichle, J., Ratcliff, A. & Esser, J. (1994). Effects of selection techniques and array sizes on short term visual memory. *Augmentative and Alternative Communication, 10,* 237-244.

National Research Council (2001). *Educating Children With Autism.* Committee on Educational Interventions for Children with Autism. Catherine Lord and James P. McGee, eds. Division of Behavioral and Social Sciences and Education. Washington, DC: National Academy Press.

National Research Council (1999). *How People Learn: Brain, Mind, Experience, and School.* Washington, DC: National Academy Press.

Reed, P., Bowser, G. & Korsten, J. (2002). *How Do You Know It? How Can You Show It? Making Assistive Technology Decisions.* Oshkosh, WI: The Wisconsin Assistive Technology Initiative.

Reed, P. *The Wisconsin Assistive Technology Initiative Assessment Package.* Retrieved from http://www.wati.org

Reichle, J., Dettling, E.E., Drager, K.D.R. & Leiter, A. (2000). A comparison of correct responses and response latency for fixed and dynamic displays: Performance of a learner with severe developmental disabilities. *Augmentative and Alternative Communication, 16*(3), 154-163. Taylor & Francis.

Romski, M.A. & Sevcik, R.A. (1992). Developing augmented language in children with severe mental retardation. In S. Warren & J. Reichle, (eds.), *Causes and Effects in Communication and Language Intervention* (pp.113-130). Baltimore, MD: Paul H. Brooks.

Romski, M.A. & Sevcik, R.A. (1996). *Breaking the Speech Barrier: Language Development Through Augmented Means.* Baltimore: Paul H. Brooks.

Romski, M.A., Sevcik, R.A. & Adamson, L.B. (1999). Communication patterns of youth with mental retardation with and without their speech-output communication devices. *American Journal on Mental Retardation, 104,* 249-259.

Rowland, C. & Schweigert, P. (2000). Tangible symbols, tangible outcomes. *AAC: Augmentative and Alternative Communication, 16*(2), 61-78.

Rowland, C. & Schweigert, P. (1990). *Tangible Symbol Systems: Symbolic Communication for Individuals with Multisensory Impairments.* Tucson, AZ: Communication Skill Builders.

Rubin, S. (Screenwriter) & Wurzburg, G. (Director) (2004). *Autism Is a World.* Washington, DC: State of the Art, Inc.

Schepis, M., Reid, D., Behrmann, M., & Sutton, K. (1998). Increasing communicative interactions of young children with autism using a voice output communication aid and naturalistic teaching. *Journal of Applied Behavior Analysis, 31,* 561-578.

Schwartz, I., Garfinkle, A. & Bauer, J. (1998). The Picture Exchange Communication System: Communication Outcomes for Young Children with Disabilities. *Topics in Early Childhood Special Education, 18,* 144-159.

Sheldon, J. & Hager, R. (2004). Funding of assistive technology to make work a reality: Funding for Work-Related Assistive Technology Through Special Education Programs, State Vocational Rehabilitation Agencies, Medicaid, Medicare and SSI's Plan for Achieving Self Support. Buffalo, NY: National Assistive Technology Advocacy Project. Available online at http://www.nls.org.

Sigafoos, J. (1999). Creating opportunities for augmentative and alternative communication: Strategies for involving people with developmental disabilities. *AAC: Augmentative and Alternative Communication, 15*(3), 183-190.

Zabala, J. (2000). *The SETT Framework.* Retrieved from http://www.joyzabala.com.

Resource Guide

AAC-Related Organizations & Websites

American Speech-Language-
  Hearing Association (ASHA)
10801 Rockville Pike
Rockville, MD 20852
(800) 638-8255
www.asha.org

Association of Assistive Technology
  Act Programs (ATAP)
P.O. Box 32
Delmar, NY 12054
(518) 439-1263
www.ataporg.org

Augmentative Communication
  Consultants, Inc. (ACCI)
P.O. Box 731
Moon Township, PA 15108
(412) 264-6121   (800) 982-2248
www.acciinc.com

California State University Northridge
  (CSUN) Center on Disabilities
18111 Nordhoff St.
Northridge, CA 91330-8340
(818) 677-2684
www.csun.edu/cod

Closing the Gap
526 Main Street
P.O. Box 68
Henderson, MN 56044
(507) 248-3294
www.closingthegap.com

Council for Exceptional Children
  (CEC) & Public Policy Homepage
1110 North Glebe Rd., Suite 300
Arlington, VA 22201-5704
(888) CEC-SPED
www.cec.sped.org;
www.cec.sped.org/pp
Updates on special education law:
www.ideapractices.org

International Society for
  Augmentative and Alternative
  Communication (ISAAC)
49 The Donway West, Suite 308
Toronto, ON M3C 3M9
Canada
(416) 385-0351
www.isaac-online.org

National Association of Protection and
Advocacy Systems, Inc. (NAPAS)
900 Second St. NE, Suite 211
Washington, DC 20002
(202) 408-9514
www.napas.org

National Center on Workforce and
Disability/Adult-Institute for
Community Inclusion
UMass Boston
100 Morrissey Blvd.
Boston, MA 02125
(888) 886-9898
www.onestops.info

Neighborhood Legal Services, Inc.
(NLS) & The National Assistive
Technology Advocacy Project
295 Main St., Room 495
Buffalo, NY 14203
(716) 847-0650
www.nls.org

Quality Indicators for Assistive
Technology (QIAT)
(Internet address only)
www.qiat.org

Rehabilitation Engineering and
Assistive Technology Society of
North America (RESNA)
1700 N. Moore St., Suite 1540
Arlington, VA 22209-1903
(703) 524-6686
www.resna.org

U.S. Dept. of Education Website
(Internet address only)
www.ed.gov

U.S. Society for Augmentative and
Alternative Communication
(USSAAC)
P.O. Box 21418
Sarasota, FL 34276
(941) 925-8875
www.ussaac.org

Wisconsin Assistive Technology
Initiative (WATI)
Polk Library
800 Algoma Blvd.
Oshkosh, WI 54901
(920) 424-2247   (800) 991-5576
www.wati.org

AAC Products

AAC Interventions
916 W. Castillo Dr.
Litchfield Park, AZ 85340
or
W4855 Hemlock Road
Mondovi, WI 54755
E-mail: julie@aacintervention.com;
carmussel@cox.net
www.aacintervention.com

AbleNet, Inc.
2808 Fairview Ave.
Roseville, MN 55113-1308
(800) 322-0956
www.ablenetinc.com

Adaptivation, Inc.
2225 W. 50th St., Suite 100
Sioux Falls, SD 57105
(605) 335-4445   (800) 723-2783
www.adaptivation.com

AlphaSmart, Inc.
973 University Ave.
LosGatos, CA 95032
(888) 274-0680
www.alphasmart.com

Attainment Company, Inc.
P.O. Box 930160
Verona, WI 53593-0160
(800) 327-4269
www.attainmentcompany.com

Augmentative Communication, Inc.
   (ACI)
One Surf Way, #237
Monterey, CA 93940
(831) 649-3050
www.augcominc.com

Creative Communicating
P.O. Box 3358
Park City, UT 84060
(435) 645-7737
www.creativecommunicating.com

Don Johnston, Inc.
26799 West Commerce Dr.
Volo, IL 60073
(800) 999-4660
www.donjohnston.com

DynaVox Technologies
2100 Wharton St., Suite 400
Pittsburgh, PA 15203
(888) 697-7332;
(866) 396-2869
www.dynavoxsystems.com

Enkidu Research
2100 Wharton St., Suite 400
Pittsburgh, PA 15203
(800) 344-1778
www.enkidu.net

IntelliTools
1720 Corporate Circle
Petaluma, CA 94954-6924
(707) 773-2000   (800) 899-6687
www.intellitools.com

Mayer-Johnson LLC
P.O. Box 1579
Solana Beach, CA 92075-7579
(858) 550-0084   (800) 588-4548
www.mayer-johnson.com

Prentke-Romich Co.
1022 Heyl Rd.
Wooster, OH 44691
(330) 262-1984   (800) 262-1984
www.prentrom.com

Pyramid Educational Consultants,
   Inc.
226 West Park Place, Suite 1
Newark, DE 19711
(302) 368-2515   (888) 732-7462
www.pecs.com

Saltillo Corporation
2143 TR112
Millersburg, OH 44654
(330) 674-6722   (800) 382-8622
www.saltillo.com

Semantic Compaction Systems
   (SCS)
1000 Killarney Dr.
Pittsburgh, PA 15234
(412) 885-8541
www.minspeak.com

Simplified Technology for Children
with Disabilities
LJ Burkhart
6201 Candle Ct.
Eldersburg, MD 21784
E-mail: linda@Lburkhart.com
www.lburkhart.com/main.htm;
www.lburkhart.com

Slater Software, Inc.
351 Badger Ln.
Guffey, CO 80820
(719) 479-2255   (877) 306-6968
www.slatersoftware.com

Words+, Inc.
1220 W. Avenue J
Lancaster, CA 93534-2902
(800) 869-8521
www.words-plus.com

Zygo Industries, Inc.
P.O. Box 1008
Portland, OR 97207
(800) 234-6006
www.zygo-usa.com

AAC Conferences

Assistive Technology Industry
Association (ATIA)
401 N. Michigan Ave.
Chicago, IL 60611-4267
(312) 321-5172   (877) 687-2842
www.atia.org

California State University
Northridge (CSUN) Center on
Disabilities
18111 Nordhoff St.
Northridge, CA 91330-8340
(818) 677-2578
www.csun.edu/cod

Closing the Gap
526 Main St.
P.O. Box 68
Henderson, MN 56044
(507) 248-3294
www.closingthegap.com

Communication Aid Manufacturers Association (CAMA)
205 West Randolph, Suite 1830
Chicago, IL 60606
(800) 441-2262
www.aacproducts.org

International Society for
Augmentative and Alternative
Communication (ISAAC)
49 The Donway West, Suite 308
Toronto, ON M3C 3M9
Canada
(416) 385-0351
www.isaac-online.org

Southeast Augmentative Communication Conference (SEAC)
2430 11th Ave. North
Birmingham, AL 35234
(205) 251-0165
E-mail: seac@ucpbham.com

U.S. Society for Augmentative
and Alternative Communication
(USSAAC)
P.O. Box 21418
Sarasota, FL 34276
(941) 925-8875
www.ussaac.org

AAC-Related Journals & Newsletters

*Augmentative and Alternative
Communication (AAC) Journal*
Decker Periodicals, Inc.
4 Hughson St. South, 4th Floor
P.O. 620, LCD 1
Hamilton, Ontario L8N 3K7
Canada
(905) 522-7017
www.isaac-online.org;
www.bcdecker.com

*Augmentative Communication News
(ACN)*
One Surf Way, # 237
Monterey, CA 93940
(831) 649-3050
www.augcominc.com/acn.html

Closing the Gap Newspaper
526 Main St.
P.O. Box 68
Henderson, MN 56044
(507) 248-3294
www.closingthegap.com

*Focus on Autism and Developmental
Disorders*
PRO-ED Journals
8700 Shoal Creek Blvd.
Austin, TX 78757-6897
(800) 897-3202
www.proedinc.com

Journal of Autism and
Developmental Disorders
233 Spring St. Fl 7
New York, NY 10013-1522
(212) 620-8027
www.springeronline.com

Speak Up
Newsletter of the U.S. Augmentative and Alternative Communication Association (USAAC)
P.O. Box 21418
Sarasota, FL 34276
(941) 925-8875
www.ussaac.org

Glossary

AAC. *See* Augmentative & Alternative Communication.

AAC Service. *See* Assistive Technology Service.

ADA. *See* Americans with Disabilities Act.

Aided AAC System. *AAC* that requires an external tool, other than the communicator's body; namely, a *communication board*, keyboard, *VOCA*, or pencil and paper. *See also* Unaided AAC System.

Aided Language Stimulation. *Receptive language* training in which the speaking *communication partner* pairs speech with pointing to symbols. There is the expectation, but not the pressure, for the non-speaking communicator to respond.

Alphabet Board. A *no-tech communication board* with letters of the alphabet. *Communication partners* use it for both giving and receiving *communication*.

Americans with Disabilities Act (ADA). Federal law that states individuals with disabilities must be afforded the same opportunities to participate in our society and obtain the same benefit from that participation as their peers without disabilities.

ASD. *See* Autism Spectrum Disorder.

Asperger's Disorder. A pervasive developmental disorder characterized by better-developed early language and cognitive skills, but also an inability to interact appropriately in social situations. *See also* Autism Spectrum Disorder.

Assistive Technology (AT). Any item, piece of equipment, product or system, either acquired commercially or modified, that is used to increase, maintain, or improve the capability of people with disabilities.

Assistive Technology Act (ATA). Federal legislation reauthorized in 2004 that provides funding for *assistive technology (AT)* programs and addresses the *AT* needs of individuals from birth through adulthood.

Assistive Technology Service. By law, services include evaluation, providing the tool or device, training the student, staff, and parents, modifying, repairing, replacing the device, and evaluating effectiveness at each *IEP* meeting.

Assistive Technology Team. An interdisciplinary team of professionals that provides support services through evaluations, expertise, and training to parents and school staff members for students with disabilities whose needs are not being met with current *interventions* and who may benefit from the use of technology.

AT. *See* Assistive Technology.

ATA. *See* Assistive Technology Act.

Augmentative & Alternative Communication (AAC). Any tool, device, picture, word, symbol, or gesture that enhances, clarifies, and improves existing *expressive* and *receptive language*.

Autism. *See* Autism Spectrum Disorder.

Autism Spectrum Disorder (ASD). A pervasive developmental disorder characterized by disabilities is social interaction, language acquisition and use, thinking skills, and odd or unusual mannerisms, behaviors, and habits.

Cell. The visual boundary (usually square or rectangle) that encloses a symbol on a *communication board* or *VOCA*.

Communication. Speech, body language, facial expressions, gestures, and written language or print. *See also* Expressive Language; Receptive Language.

Communication Binder/Wallet. A variety of activity and environmentally specific *communication boards* in a portable book or folder.

Communication Board. A *no-tech AAC* system consisting of pictures, photos, or words, specific to an activity and used for interactive *expressive* and *receptive communication*. Also called *language board*.

Communication Overlay. *See* Overlay Grid.

Communication Partner. Speaking or non-speaking communicator who gives and receives information through conventional *communication* techniques and *AAC*.

Communicative Input. Visual or auditory *communication* produced from speech, pointing to symbols, or generated by a *VOCA* and received by the *communication partner*. *See also* Communicative Output; Input.

Communicative Output. Visual or auditory *communication* produced from speech, pointing to symbols, or generated by a *VOCA* and sent to a *communication partner*. *See also* Communicative Input.

Complex Cue. Multiple-step direction or a combination of stimuli that are difficult for people with *ASD* to understand, and can sometimes be aversive. Also called *multiple cue*. *See also* Multiple Cue Responding.

Cue. *See* Prompt.

Dynamic Display Device. *High-tech AAC* device with multiple *communication* levels that change by activating a touch screen.

Early Intervention. The specialized way of interacting with infants and toddlers to minimize the effects of conditions that can delay early development. *See also* Intervention. *See also* Individualized Family Service Plan.

Early Intervention Team. A team of trained professionals who provide specialized services for infants and toddlers who are at risk for, or showing signs of, developmental delay. *See also* Early Intervention; Individualized Family Service Plan; Intervention.

Early & Periodic Screening, Diagnosis, and Treatment (EPSDT). Federal law requiring periodic screening, diagnosis, and medically necessary treatment services to all people receiving *Medicaid*.

Engineered Environment. An environment deliberately structured for *communication* opportunities, including activity-specific *communication boards* and physical rearrangements to prompt *communication*.

EPSDT. *See* Early & Periodic Screening, Diagnosis, and Treatment.

Expressive Language. Outgoing language that is generated by speech, pointing to or exchanging a symbol or word, or keyboarding that is received by another person. *See also* Communicative Output; Receptive Language.

Facilitated Communication. A technique by which a facilitator supports the hand or arm of a communicatively impaired individual while using a keyboard or typing device.

FAPE. *See* "Free Appropriate Public Education."

FBA. *See* Functional Behavioral Assessment.

FCT with AAC. *See* Functional Communication Training with AAC.

"Free Appropriate Public Education" (FAPE). The right, under *IDEA*, of every child with disabilities to an education provided at public expense that is appropriate to his or her developmental strengths and needs.

Functional Behavior Assessment (FBA). A problem-solving process using a variety of techniques and strategies to identify the purposes, or functions, of specific problem behavior so that appropriate *interventions* can be designed.

Functional Communication Training with AAC (FCT with AAC). A protocol designed to decrease problem behaviors by first determining why a particular behavior is occurring, or what a person is trying to convey with the problem behavior; and second, replacing that behavior with a more appropriate way to communicate.

Functional Spontaneous Communication. *Communication* that is unprompted and elicits a desired effect. It is a critically important skill for a person with *ASD* and a predictor of high quality of life outcomes.

High-tech AAC. Sophisticated voice *output* systems with computer mechanisms with the capability of generating complex *communication*. *See also* Dynamic Display Device; Iconic Coding Device; Voice Output Communication Aid.

Hyperlexia. A syndrome in which a child has a precocious ability to read words but does not understand much of what he reads.

Iconic Coding Device. A sophisticated *AAC* device that uses coded symbol combinations, based on specific rules that often involve understanding abstract concepts, to generate messages.

IDEA. *See* Individuals with Disabilities Education Act.

IDEA 2004. *See* Individuals with Disabilities Education Improvement Act of 2004.

IDEIA. *See* Individuals with Disabilities Education Improvement Act of 2004.

IEP. *See* Individualized Education Program.

IEP Team. The group of parents, family members, special and general educators, *speech and language pathologists*, and other support services members, such as *occupational and physical therapists*, that meets regularly to review a child's *IEP*.

IFSP. *See* Individualized Family Service Plan.

IHP. *See* Individualized Habilitation Program.

Individualized Education Program (IEP). The written plan that specifies the services the local education agency has agreed to provide a child with disabilities who is eligible under *IDEA*; for children ages three to twenty-one. *See also* IEP Team.

Individualized Family Service Plan (IFSP). A federally mandated written document that guides the *early intervention* process for infants and toddlers, birth to age three, with disabilities. *See also* Early Intervention Team.

Individualized Habilitation Program (IHP). A federally mandated written document that details the daily living, behavioral, and vocational program of people with disabilities who are recipients of *Medicaid* support.

Individuals with Disabilities Education Act (IDEA). Federal law that ensures that every student with a disability is provided a *free and appropriate public education* in the *least restrictive environment*. *IDEA* also requires that *assistive technology* be considered for all students at each *IEP* meeting.

Individuals with Disabilities Education Improvement Act of 2004 (IDEIA). Federal law that reauthorized and amended *IDEA* in 2004. Regulations to be written in 2005.

Input. Information that a person receives through any of the senses (sight, hearing, touch, taste, smell) that helps that person develop new skills. *See also* Communicative Input; Communicative Output; Prompt.

Insistence On Sameness. A tendency in many people with *ASD* to become upset when familiar routines or environments are changed.

Intervention. Action taken to improve a person's potential for success by compensating for a delay or deficit in their physical, emotional, or mental functioning. *See also* Early Intervention; Early Intervention Team.

Joint Attention. The ability to coordinate attention between a person and an object. When a child shows a toy to a parent or *communication partner*, or points to something of interest, she is demonstrating joint attention.

Language Board. *See* Communication Board.

Least Restrictive Environment. The requirement under *IDEA* that children receiving special education must be educated to the fullest extent possible with children who do not have disabilities.

Low-tech AAC. *Voice output communication aids* with simple electronic components that have the capability of less than eight minutes of speech.

Manual Sign. A form of *unaided AAC*, manual signing is visual or tactile *communication* given and received through various movements and positions of the arms, hands, and face. Also called *sign language*.

Mediation. Under *IDEA*, when parents and school officials meet with a neutral third party to discuss a mutually acceptable resolution to a formal complaint.

Medicaid. Federal and state programs that provide medically necessary services and equipment for people with disabilities.

Medical Assistance. *See* Medicaid.

Motor. Relating to the ability to use muscles to move oneself.

Multiple Cue. *See* Complex Cue.

Multiple Cue Responding. The natural ability of typically developing children that involves recognizing and understanding the many sensory components of an object, person, task, or request, and integrating them into a meaningful experience or *cue. See also* Complex Cue.

NAL. *See* Natural Aided Language.

Natural Aided Language (NAL). A measurable and quantifiable interactive, *receptive* and *expressive language intervention* in which the speaking *communication partner* provides *receptive language input* by pairing speech with pointing to visual symbols.

No-tech AAC. Non-electronic *AAC* tools with symbols or words on common materials, such as laminated card-stock. *See also* Communication Board; Visual Schedule.

Occupational Therapist (OT). A therapist who specializes in improving the development of fine *motor* and adaptive skills.

OT. *See* Occupational Therapist.

Output. *See* Communicative Output.

Overlay Grid. A single page or display on an *AAC* tool or device with one or more visual symbols representing a specific message or activity. *See also* Voice Output Communication Aid.

Participation Model. An *AAC* assessment and *intervention* tool developed by Beukelman & Mirenda that identifies and plans opportunities for participation and *communication* by considering the practices of a student's same-aged, non-disabled peers.

PCS. *See* Picture Communication Symbols©.

PDD-NOS. *See* Pervasive Developmental Disorder-Not Otherwise Specified.

PECS. *See* Picture Exchange Communication System.

Perseveration. Seemingly purposeless repetitive movement or speech that is thought to be motivated by a person's inner preoccupations. Also called *stereotypy. See also* Self-Stimulation.

Pervasive Developmental Disorder-Not Otherwise Specified (PDD-NOS). One of the five subcategories of *ASD* characterized by severe and pervasive impairment in social and *communication* skills, or *stereotyped* behavior, interests, or activities. This category describes people who show some of the symptoms of a particular *ASD* diagnosis, but not all.

Physical Therapist (PT). A therapist who specializes in improving the development of *motor* skills, particularly the coordination of gross *motor* activities.

Picture Communication Symbols© (PCS). Most widely used (within the U.S.) line drawings of actions, objects, and descriptors used as the basis for pictorial visual language. Developed by Mayer-Johnson LLC.

Picture Exchange Communication System (PECS). A systematic procedure (developed by Andy Bondy and Lori Frost) of teaching a child to initiate *communication* based on exchanging a picture of a desired object for that object. The process goes on to teach discrimination of symbols and then how to put them all together in simple sentences.

Prompt. *Input* that encourages an individual to perform a movement or activity. Also called *cue*. *See also* Prompt Dependence; Prompt Fading; Prompt Hierarchy.

Prompt Dependence. When an individual requires a *prompt* in order to perform a taught task or behavior. *See also* Prompt Fading; Prompt Hierarchy.

Prompt Fading. The process by which a *prompt* is gradually removed over time until it is no longer provided. *See also* Prompt Dependence; Prompt Hierarchy.

Prompt Hierarchy. A systematic method of *prompting*, or *cueing* a person in order to help him learn a new skill. A *prompt* can be natural, point, gesture, model, verbal, or physical. The hierarchy can be sequenced from least directive to most directive or visa-versa. *See also* Prompt Dependence; Prompt Fading.

PT. *See* Physical Therapist.

Receptive Language. Language that is received and understood through sound, sight, or touch. *See also* Communicative Input; Expressive Language; Input.

Rehabilitation Act of 1973. *See* Section 504; Section 508.

Representational Symbol System. A form of *aided AAC* that utilizes two-dimensional symbols, including photographs or line-drawings. *See also* Tangible Symbol System.

SAL. *See* System for Augmenting Language.

Section 504. Part of the Rehabilitation Act of 1973, amended in 1993, Section 504 prohibits any federal agency, including public schools, from discriminating against a person because of a disability and requires "reasonable accommodations."

Section 508. Part of the Rehabilitation Act of 1973, amended in 1993, Section 508 of this law requires federal agencies to make electronic and information technology accessible to people with disabilities.

Self -Stimulation. The act of providing physical, visual, or auditory stimulation for oneself; rocking back and forth or repeatedly pressing a key on a keyboard are examples. Also called *stimming. See also* Perseveration.

SETT Framework. An ongoing *AAC* planning tool developed by Zabala whereby the *AAC* user's team identifies each of the SETT components to design the *AAC intervention*. SETT stands for Student, Environment, Task, Tools.

Sign Language. *See* Manual Signs.

SLP. *See* Speech and Language Pathologist.

Social Networks. An *AAC* assessment tool developed by Blackstone & Berg that considers the social relationships of a potential *AAC* user and how to identify and foster *communication* opportunities within those networks.

Speech and Language Pathologist (SLP). A therapist who works to improve speech and language skills, as well as to improve oral *motor* abilities.

Speech Generating Device. *See* Voice Output Communication Aid (VOCA).

Stereotypy. *See* Perseveration.

Stimming. *See* Self-Stimulation.

System for Augmenting Language (SAL). An *AAC* strategy wherein the speaking *communication partner* uses a *VOCA* to provide *communicative input* and *output* to their non-speaking *communication partner* in natural settings.

Tactile Symbol. *See* Tangible Symbol System.

Tangible Symbol System. A form of *aided AAC* that utilizes three-dimensional objects, partial objects, or miniature objects, textured symbols, or adapted line-drawn symbols with raised contours that can be identified by touch. Also called *tactile symbols*, these are used with people who have visual or cognitive deficits and for whom the line-drawn symbols are too abstract. *See also* Representational Symbol System.

Telecommunications Act of 1996. Law that requires manufacturers of telecommunication equipment to ensure that equipment is accessible to people with disabilities.

Unaided AAC System. *Communication* that involves the use of the physical body with no external tools or devices, such as vocalizations, gestures, facial expressions, body language. *See also* Aided AAC System; Manual Sign.

Visual Cueing Tool. Symbols, *manual signs*, or written words used to augment verbal instructions and *prompts*.

Visual Schedule. A kind of *no-tech* visual tool using objects, photographs, line drawings, or words representing specific activities and arranged linearly according to when these activities occur.

VOCA. *See* Voice Output Communication Aid.

Vocabulary Inventory. A list of nouns, verbs, and descriptors that are typically used in a particular activity.

Voice Output Communication Aid (VOCA). An electronic *communication* device with the capability of producing speech when specific buttons or *cells* are activated. The speech may be digitized, recorded, or synthesized. Also known as a *speech generating device*. A *VOCA* is considered durable medical equipment by *Medicaid*.

WATI. *See* Wisconsin Assistive Technology Initiative.

Wisconsin Assistive Technology Initiative (WATI). A comprehensive assessment tool developed by Reed that guides the *assistive technology team* in considering not only *AAC* for *communication*, but also literacy supports.

Index

About the Author

Joanne M. Cafiero, Ph.D., is an autism and AAC practitioner and trainer. She was transformed by her relationships with people with autism while working at Bittersweet Farms Autistic Community in Whitehouse, Ohio. It was at Bittersweet Farms that Dr. Cafiero learned the importance of contextually-based, meaningful learning experiences for people on the autism spectrum.

Dr. Cafiero was a member of the National Academy of Sciences Committee on Educational Interventions for Children with Autism and Autism Projects Director for Johns Hopkins University Center for Technology in Education. As a faculty member of Johns Hopkins School of Professional Studies, she co-designed the Johns Hopkins graduate program, "Teaching Children with Autism."

As an instructor, Dr. Cafiero has taught adolescents with autism in public schools and developed and taught an AAC class for students with severe communication challenges. Currently, Dr. Cafiero is doing research in AAC and autism in the context of the school, community, and family. She provides training and support in developing meaningful communication and participation programs for individuals with autism in the U.S., Europe, and Asia.